PRAISE FOR

Down Home Wisdom:
Faith, Freedom, and The Front Porch Way of Life.

"Andy Hollifield's inspirational gift of storytelling is as welcoming as a rocking chair pushed by a cool southern breeze on a warm summer night. His timeless, homespun stories invite us to shake off life's cares and revisit the front porch of yesteryear—a place where life slows, friendships deepen, and stories linger. Whether reminding us that nice moments stick like sticky notes or that broken crayons still color, each refreshing tale is a timeless morsel that tugs on our heartstrings and beckons us to stay awhile. Won't you join me? Andy left the lights on for us."

—Starr Ayers, third-generation artist and multiple award-winning author of *For the Love of Emma* and *Waiting for Sunset*

"*Down Home Wisdom* is like a pat on the back from Grandpa or a favorite uncle. It's like hearing them say, "Did I ever tell you about the time…" and later you walk away feeling better about the world than when you came in. This book is full of simple truths that aren't as simple to some as they used to be. Through charming short stories, the book teaches about the value of hard work, the importance of integrity, the power of kindness, and other Bible-based life lessons."

—Heather Norman Smith, award-winning author of *Songs for a Sunday* and *A Simple Kindness in Flatsboro*

"Set your glass of sweet tea down on the side table, pull up your rocker, and set to rockin'. These wonderful tales from *Down Home Wisdom,* written in Andy's signature straightforward mountain-speak, will have you swearing you're sitting with him on his front porch, waving at the passers-by, as he entertains you with story after story. If you are feeling nostalgic, you'll love this book!"

—Lori Marett, Writing Coach, Screenwriter, and Director of the Gideon Film Festival

"When you read Andy's book, you feel as if you've gained another friend who really wants the best for you. He's a man's man who still relates to women. I appreciate his humor, down-to-earth wisdom, and practical faith. This book is a win!"

—Anthony Kirk Hayes, Ordained Minister, Retired U.S. Army Chief Warrant Officer Four, B.S. in Psychology with an Emphasis in Life Coaching

DOWN HOME STORIES

Faith, Freedom, and the Front Porch Way of Life

Andy Hollifield

Down Home Wisdom: Faith, Freedom, and the Front Porch Way of Life, Andy Hollifield
Issued in electronic and paperback formats
Paperback ISBN: 979-8-9897467-9-8
E-book ISBN: 978-1-970354-00-3
LCCN: 2025922555
First Edition

Publisher: Dressed in Love Press, LLC
www.drkatherinehayes.com

Cover Designer: Katherine Hutchinson-Hayes
Book Interior Designer: Jenifer Jennings

Printed in the United States of America

This book is dedicated first to God, who gave me the ability to write. Also, to my parents who have always encouraged me to chase my dreams and do my best at everything I do. My sisters, just for being my sisters, and my big brother Jim, whose gift of a kidney transplant gave me a second chance at life. Without his selfless gift, I probably wouldn't have been alive to write this book. He will always be my hero.

Table of Contents

Eleven stories about things that are truly priceless.

Seven stories showing the fallacy of judging others.

FOREWORD

I was born and raised in the Appalachian Mountains. My mother was one of seven children. I recall the hot summer weekends when her siblings and their families would all gather at Mamaw's house to can beans, make apple butter, and shuck corn. Although we kids had to pull our share of the workload, what made it bearable was when my uncles began to tell stories. Some were fun, some nonsense, but many times these stories had hidden life lessons. We learned while we listened. My grandma used to tell these same types of tales on the porch after supper. She'd pull me onto her lap, press my head against her chest, and sway with me in the giant pine rocker. As she rocked, she'd tell me stories from her childhood that offered these same practical life lessons. She'd chuckle and say, "Now, you do as I say, not as I do. Don't want you learnin' the hard way like me."

Story has long been the most effective communication we have at our fingertips. Children relate to stories. These tales help them process the life around them and teach them skills they might otherwise miss. It's never been a secret that God has always been an important part of life for the mountain people who inhabit this area. On any given Sunday, you would see folks make the trek to the church where they worshiped. It only made sense that this same faith would follow them home to their front porches.

The world pushes us to pare down, take the thought out of our actions, and this waters down the truth. Fewer and fewer grandparents have the opportunity to rock their grandchildren on the porch as the sun eases behind the mountains. Life is so busy that we often overlook the precious moments when we can instill Biblical truths through storytelling.

Many times, life in the mountains is looked upon as slow and uneducated, but the truth is, those raised in the hills and hollars are gifted with a wisdom far beyond the average. *Down Home Wisdom – Faith, Freedom, and Front Porch Way of Life* drives home that gentle mountain way of teaching—through story. Simple stories. Just as Jesus taught through parables, Andy Hollifield brings his own mountain joy to the front porch rocker. His stories are sweet, tell-it-like-it-is tales that teach, convict, and show the gentler side of people. These sweet and endearing tales within the covers of this book will remind you of a God who stands inches away, watching, loving, and guiding your steps.

Pull up a rocker. Kick off your shoes and rest your feet on the porch rail. Lean back and remember, then take these warm and tender stories to everyone you know. Slip into the mountains and the front porch way of life, and then soak in the wisdom of when story and scripture walk hand in hand.

—Cindy K. Sproles, cofounder of Christian Devotions Ministries and best-selling author of *Coal Black Lies* and *This is Where it Ends*

INTRODUCTION

This book is written for families and people of all ages. The intent is to share timeless wisdom and Scripture that many of us older folks grew up with. These principles were not only taught but also modeled in the lives of the adults around us. Back in my day, down home, it was up to us as children, teenagers, and young adults to build character by living out these wise words. Many of them were just old sayings to us until we got older and realized we were now those older people who tried to drive home these morals through sometimes thick skulls.

One day, we were dealing with Little League and scouting, thinking about what position we wanted to play or how hard we were willing to work for our badges. The next day, we were deciding where, or if, we would go to college, sign up for the military, or join the workforce. The decisions became bigger as we grew older, and the consequences became more substantial. We were taught to think for ourselves. With that responsibility came the need to justify our positions, think rationally through decisions, and have the dignity to own the outcome, be it good or bad.

From the fields and courts of the youth league, we were taught the ultimate principle of sportsmanship. Once explained to us, it was a vital quality to display if we wanted to continue participating. That meant playing well with others and treating them with the same respect we expected from them. No matter how intense our personalities, we were reminded that the competition was only a game to be enjoyed, because those teaching us knew Father Time would one day steal our ability and prowess.

Sportsmanship went far beyond the athletic field and gymnasiums and became the fabric of who we were. We learned how to treat others in general and how to respond when situations didn't turn out as we would have liked. How to deal with disappointment and show compassion for others who were dealing with adverse circumstances were among the most impactful lessons we learned. Our behavior was largely defined by the adages taught in our formative years. Children are taught everything from the alphabet, counting, nursery rhymes, and Bible stories through constant repetition. These adages taught us respect, courtesy, and manners. They became the ingrained qualities that shaped our character.

Regardless of where or what we were doing, the cardinal sin was backtalking an adult. Judgment was handed down in short order, especially if we were within arm's reach. Back then, our participation in activities other than church always depended directly on our behavior. We weren't allowed to behave like hooligans at home, much less anywhere else.

We swore to ourselves we would do things differently when we became parents. Instead, we realize we've become a younger version of our parents, and we pray daily that God will give us half the wisdom they had when we were growing up. They indeed get smarter the older we get.

The stories in this book emphasize issues that are not only

important for children but also for adults: honesty, friendship, overcoming adversity, and believing in oneself, to name a few. They also highlight the need to believe in others at any age and thereby encourage them to always put forth their best effort, regardless of what they're doing. The stories illustrate that despite our mistakes or shortcomings, we can rise above circumstances and achieve success. Success isn't defined by wealth or prestige but by the qualities that make us who we are.

I hope you enjoy the book and impart some of its lessons, wisdom, and old sayings to someone who can use them. This book is intended to interest children and young adults. I hope it can serve as a tool for older folks to impart the lessons to young people that many of us learned growing up, without even realizing how they were shaping our lives. This isn't only a book of adages and heartwarming stories, but also a bit of insight into how life was when I was growing up *DOWN HOME*.

—*Andy Hollifield*

NEVER STOP BELIEVING IN YOURSELF

Ten stories to encourage anyone to always believe in themselves.

"You know you can't do that." How many times have you heard someone say that to you? The statement is often followed by a list of reasons someone feels you're incapable of the task you're attempting. Folks don't always think about how their comments and opinions may hurt or discourage you. Believing in yourself and having faith to face the outcome of your decisions becomes much harder when operating under a cloud of doubt and discouragement.

As a youngster, I played three years of baseball, accumulating no hits, no runs, and numerous errors. I sprained my knee twice within two weeks after sliding into home plate and being tagged out. I still came to practice every day because I loved the camaraderie. The fact that I was there encouraging my teammates earned me their respect, regardless of my lack of ability. Now, in my golden years when I see my teammates, they still call me by my baseball nickname, Sparky.

In my one year of basketball, I rode the pine, as being a benchwarmer was called back then. I touched the ball once in one game all season and was immediately penalized for traveling. Football was my best sport. I was a neighborhood superstar, but I was too small to be a defensive lineman on my youth league team.

My short-lived athletic career wasn't a complete waste of time—

quite the opposite. I learned about the sportsmanship Dad always harped at my brother and me about. I learned a lot about what it meant by watching those who didn't have any and began to see its importance.

In sixth grade, I turned to music and joined the band and chorus. I sang at church, so it was a natural fit. I signed up to be a drummer. By my junior year, I played the tri-toms in the marching band and was fair but not great. I was carrying the coolest drums, at least in my mind. Classmates cheered when we marched by.

I didn't write this to brag about my mediocrity in sports or music. I wrote it as an example that believing in yourself doesn't always mean you're better than anyone else at what you do. Many successful athletes haven't been good teammates. Even accomplished musicians, actors, or other professionals have allowed success to go to their heads, failed miserably, and are soon forgotten. Greatness isn't about ability but passion. I wasn't very good at any sports on organized teams. I didn't achieve stardom in music. I did, however, have a strong belief in myself because I was passionate about whatever I did.

I hope the following stories encourage you to always believe in yourself. Many people have achieved greatness because someone else believed in them, even though they didn't believe in themselves at first. Being passionate about whatever you do is priority one. Attending practice requires passion, especially when your knee hurts or you rarely play. You must be passionate to excel in whatever you do. You don't always have to be the best, but be eager enough to be your best and never stop believing in yourself.

THE BASKETBALL

*For whatsoever is born of God overcometh the
world: and this is the victory that overcometh the
world, even our faith.*
—1 John 5:4 (KJV)

"Hey, runt, get you some new shoes!" Monique said as she walked
by, laughing and pointing.

Life had been tough since Angie's dad died. At only twelve years
old, she was a big sister and a part-time mom to a four-year-old. The
ghetto was rough for a single mom and her two girls. Mom worked the
second shift each night. She cleaned houses during the day when she
found work. Still, it was hand-to-mouth. New shoes weren't a priority.

Angie's family moved into government housing after her dad's
funeral. At school, no one cared that she was from a one-parent home.
Most of them were too.

Angie's only prized possession was a worn-out basketball her dad
had brought home. She often took it to the court near her apartment.
Shooting baskets was therapeutic. Although she was too short for
basketball, she still loved the game.

One day, Coach Beecher came to her in P.E. and said, "You have
potential. Why don't you try out for the team?"

"I'm too short," Angie said. "Thanks for asking, though."

"Have you ever heard of Muggsy Bogues or Spud Webb? Muggsy

was only 5'3" but holds records for steals and assists almost everywhere he played. Webb was only 5'6" but once won a slam dunk competition. They made the NBA because of their ability, despite their height. At least give it a shot."

"I can shoot, but not much else."

"I'll teach you the fundamentals," Coach Beecher replied.

Angie discovered she could play better than she thought. She walked onto the court at the team's first game wearing her worn-out sneakers.

Monique laughed at her as usual. "Look at those ridiculous shoes. Have you no shame?"

"Angie, focus on your game," Coach said. "You're not here for your shoes. You can do this. You've earned the right to be here."

"Thanks, Coach." Angie wiped the tears with her arm. All the heckling ended when Angie drained her first three-pointer, nothing but net.

"Lucky shot!" Monique shouted.

Angie's shot wasn't luck. She drained one after another. By the end of the game, she had twenty-two points and seven steals.

After the final buzzer, Coach hugged her. "I knew you could do it. You looked just like Muggsy Bogues getting those steals."

"Thanks, Coach. That was fun," she said as her teammates showered her with pats on the back.

"I'm glad your mom and sister were here. I'm proud of you, Angie. Believe in yourself."

No one, except her mom, had ever said they were proud of her.

That day changed Angie's life. She keeps those shoes in her closet as a reminder of where she came from. She now believes in herself as she heads off to college on a full-ride basketball scholarship. Before leaving, she goes to see Coach Beecher once more.

"Coach, thanks for believing in me in middle school. I wouldn't be going to college if not for you."

"Oh no, Angie. You earned it. No one gave you anything. You learned to believe in yourself and worked hard to accomplish your goals.

A little encouragement can inspire someone to make life-changing decisions.

DUSTING YOURSELF OFF

And David was greatly distressed ...
but David encouraged himself in the Lord his God.
—1 Samuel 30:6 (KJV)

With a sigh of relief, Chuck released his seatbelt, opened the door, took one step onto the fuel tank, then onto the ground. After several years of choking under pressure, he finally redeemed himself by outdriving every driver in his class except one. All the hours of practicing after work, on Saturdays, and even in the rain, paid off.

His coworker and teammate, Ronnie, ran to the truck to be the first to congratulate him.

When he exited the truck, he came out forward and hopped to the ground. He failed to come out backward using a three-point exit as required by the contest rules. That means two hands and one foot in contact with the truck until both feet are on the ground. Chuck didn't realize his mistake right away, but Ronnie did.

"I cannot believe you just did that." Ronnie groaned as he put his hands on top of his head like he was in pain.

A 25-point penalty was deducted from Chuck's score. His second-place finish was gone. He had fallen to fourth place. Chuck had worked like a man possessed, practicing for the truck rodeo, only to crash and burn.

Returning to the team tent with his head hung in disgust, Chuck apologized. "I'm sorry to let you down, guys. I did something stupid without thinking." He had only himself to blame.

For two years, Chuck lived with the anguish of knowing he had cost himself a trip to the nationals in Houston. The second-place winner went to the championship after the first-place driver was disqualified. A week in Houston, being showered with gifts, and his family getting a free vacation—all gone because of one momentary lack of concentration.

Chuck lived with his failure, occasionally being reminded of it by coworkers, but he refused to quit competing. Instead, he doubled down, worked harder, and won third place a week before the end of his career. He never went to the nationals or competed again.

Chuck didn't allow past mistakes and failures to define him. When asked why he didn't give up, he responded, "Sometimes, you just have to get up and dust yourself off."

You never fail until you quit trying.

FROM A DUCK TO A SWAN

The spirit of a man will sustain his infirmity,
but a wounded spirit who can bear?
—Proverbs 18:14 (KJV)

"I hate piano, Momma. I don't want to play anymore!" Sarah ran to her room and slammed the door. She had been taking lessons for three months and was frustrated with her lack of progress. She had worn leg braces until she was three and glasses for all her ten years. Glasses could help her see, and braces had helped her learn to walk, but there was no medical treatment for a broken spirit. While the other fourth-grade girls played basketball in the winter and soccer all summer, Sarah's mom forced her to take piano lessons. The doctors had warned her mom that rough contact with Sarah's legs would likely put her back in braces, maybe permanently.

The girls in the lunchroom showed no mercy because of Sarah's condition and leg braces. They made a pastime of teasing Sarah until she cried. Marjorie was the worst, and all the others followed her lead. Her beauty, with her long blond hair and bubbly personality, endeared her to all the other girls in the school. Sarah had tried to be friends with them, but her glasses and slight limp were magnets for ridicule, and this day was no different. Hop-a-long and Four Eyes were their favorite names for Sarah. She longed to play ball with them and fit in, but it wasn't worth the risk to her legs.

Fourteen years later, those childhood memories still hurt. As she walked onto the stage at the Metropolis Music Center in front of 3,000 people, that time of life seemed so far away. Her mom was right. The piano lessons had paid off, and she had become the pianist for the city orchestra, playing in large venues throughout the country.

After one show on a cool, rainy night, Sarah was stopped by a lady who looked like she'd lived a pretty rough life. The bags under her eyes, her stooped posture, and her callused hands indicated a hard-working woman who seemed borderline exhausted. The three kids with her were polite, but their clothes weren't fashionable by any standard. "Aren't you Sarah from just outside Abilene, Kansas?"

"Yes. Do I know you?"

"You probably wish you didn't," the lady answered. "I'm Marjorie from your fourth-grade class. When I heard you'd be here, I had to come. I owe you an apology for the way I treated you back then. When my oldest girl entered fourth grade this year with her Coke bottle glasses, I was reminded of how terrible I'd been to you. I hope you can forgive me."

"You didn't have to come here to tell me that, but thank you. Consider it forgiven," responded Sarah, stunned by this unforeseen apology.

"When I asked my daughter if she wanted to be a homecoming queen like me, she said, 'Not really.' She hopes to play the piano just like you when she grows up. Fate has a not-so-funny way of teaching us hard lessons. I never dreamed you'd be so talented, but I'm glad she has you as a role model, encouraging her to reach for the stars. The little duckling from Abilene has indeed become a graceful and beautiful swan."

Mountains are made to be climbed, conquered, or moved—
not to stop anyone from achieving their dream.

HITTING THE HIGH NOTES

He is a chosen vessel unto me
—Acts 9:15 (KJV)

The moment Sidney had waited for finally arrived. With a confident stride, she stepped to the microphone—her first opportunity to sing the national anthem to a large crowd. She hoped the endless hours of practice in front of her mirror were about to pay off.

She was a freshman, but out of everyone at the audition, she had been chosen to sing "The Star-Spangled Banner" for the opening of pregame ceremonies on homecoming night. On that warm fall night, the stadium was packed with a standing-room-only crowd. Her family was seated on the fifty-yard line directly in front of her.

After the band's drum major counted the introduction, Sidney sang the first line. Everything was perfect. She had sung in church since she was four and loved it. Then it happened. "And the rocket's red glare." She had practiced it a million times and had sung at basketball games when she was younger. But on this night, her incredible voice cracked when she hit the high note. Rattled but not deterred, she finished the song despite the tears flowing.

A few people laughed. When she exited the platform, she could barely see through her tears. One missed note had ruined the greatest night of her life. She wished she was anywhere but there. Worse yet, her mom was recording a video, and as proud moms will do, Sidney knew the most embarrassing moment of her life would be shown in perpetuity to her mom's friends as she bragged about her daughter.

Nothing could ever change that moment.

Although devastated, Sidney didn't stop singing. In her sophomore year, she joined a quartet at her church and sang with them until she received an offer from a professional group. Finally, she could live her dream.

Some of Sidney's close friends who were at the game that night teased her throughout high school. Even though they didn't mean to be cruel, they never realized how much it hurt her. In her first significant public appearance, she made a bad first impression. She would always be remembered for one wrong note.

Years later, people marveled at her incredible voice as she toured the country as a soloist. "Your voice is like that of an angel," many of her fans proclaimed. Ladies at her concerts said, "Your voice is so soothing, I play your recordings when I can't get my baby to sleep." Sidney spent the rest of her life proving that first impressions can be wrong.

God gives second chances. By His grace, anyone can overcome a bad first impression if they make their next impression better than their first.

With a lot of work and a second chance,
you can overcome a bad first impression.

THE LIFE AND TIMES OF J. W. GALION

*But when Jesus saw it, he was much displeased, and
said unto them, Suffer the little children to come
unto me, and forbid them not: for of such is the
kingdom of God.*
—Mark 10:14 (KJV)

"Man, you can play. I wish I could play like that." J. W. thanked
the young man as he signed the boy's guitar. Although he had grown
used to comments like that, he was still appreciative. He had made a
good living, seen the world, played with the biggest stars, but none of
that excited him anymore. Kids who expressed their admiration and
asked for autographs—that was a different story.

J. W. had been the young man at a concert with his guitar in hand,
and M. J. McMillan had signed his guitar even though he acted like he
didn't have time for a young fan. He'd been J. W.'s idol since he began
taking lessons at six years old. Although he left disappointed, that
night changed J. W.'s life forever. That night, he swore to himself,
"I'm gonna make it, and when I do, I'll never turn a kid away." He
had spent months doing odd jobs to buy his ticket to that concert, but
afterward, his favorite star no longer had the shine he once did.

After J. W. put his guitar case beneath the bus, someone
unexpectedly closed the door on his hand. Although the person
realized their error, the damage had been done. J. W. grimaced in pain,

wiped the blood from his throbbing hand, and noticed two of his fingertips were missing. Later, in the ER, a specialist told him, "We couldn't repair your fingers. You'll never play again."

Music was his life, and he refused to let a freak accident change that. His years of touring would end because no one wanted a picker with a mangled hand. But J. W.'s life was about to take on a whole new meaning.

After weeks of therapy and pain, J. W. spotted his guitar in the corner, waiting like an old friend. J. W. seldom heard from any of his music friends anymore. Maybe they didn't know what to say. His guitar, however, had never let him down. "Now's as good a time as any," he said to himself as he picked it up. "I learned you once, ol' gal, and I'm gonna learn you again."

As he tuned the strings for the first time in months, his love for music bubbled up in his soul. "I'm not sure how I'll ever pick with only an index finger and my pinky, but we're about to find out," he said to the guitar.

After weeks of practicing through the pain, rumors spread that J. W. was playing again. The local minor league baseball team asked him to play the national anthem at the home opener. He was thrilled someone still wanted to hear him play. The crowd gave their hometown superstar a standing ovation. Their appreciation was music to his ears. As he prepared to leave, he received a wonderful surprise. He turned to see a horde of kids with team merchandise and a six-year-old kid with a guitar bigger than he was, all wanting autographs. J. W. no longer played in arenas, but his favorite part of public appearances remained unchanged: the admiration of young kids.

J. W. returned to his roots, playing at church. The local children's hospital called and asked if he would play for their kids. Two nursing homes asked him to come and play. The mayor booked him for the county fair and the July 4th celebration were paid gigs. Thrilled to be playing again, J. W. accepted all these offers.

His mom always told him, "God's given you the talent to bless others, and He doesn't waste talent." He'd like to have a dollar for every time she had said that since the accident. In J. W.'s mind, the most remarkable result of his accident wasn't the money and lifestyle he lost, but the relationships with people he gained. He attended church regularly, and the little kids admired him, wanting to take guitar lessons.

Although he had finished physical therapy, one part of it remained—his therapist, Angela. Months of being together three times a week has benefits. Soon, they would marry in the church where they both grew up. J. W. thought he'd lost it all when that door slammed on his hand. But God had been setting him up to receive another hand, Angela's hand, in marriage.

Mom said, "God's thoughts and ways are higher than ours. This isn't the end of your career; it's the beginning of a new life."

"Was she ever right," J. W. said to himself. "Life doesn't get any better than this."

Sometimes, mistakes and accidents are God's way
of putting us on a different path.

TAKE THE STAGE

Cast not away therefore your confidence,
which hath great recompense of reward.
—Hebrews 10:35 (KJV)

Lenny Stokes loved to read but hated to memorize. His mom did all she could to ease the task of learning for him. "I'd like to be in the play at school," he said, "but I'd have to memorize all those lines. I can't do that, it's too hard."

Lennie's mom swiped her kitchen cabinet clean with a damp rag, then rested her elbows on the counter. She raised a brow. "Nothing worth having is easy, and you'll never know what you can do until you try. If you really want this, you'll have to work to learn the lines. Try your best." She kissed Lennie's head. "If you fail, at least you tried."

Tryouts for the play arrived. Lennie had worked hard every night with his mom to memorize the lines. The teacher called his name to audition. He stepped on the stage, took a deep breath, and spouted every line perfectly. The other kids clapped wildly.

For the first time in weeks, Lennie was excited to get home from school. "Mom, where are you?" he shouted as the screen door slammed shut behind him.

"I'm in the kitchen. How did the audition go, son?" she asked, not sure she wanted to hear the answer.

"I didn't miss a single word, Mom"—he paused—"I did get one

sentence out of place, but I made up a line so I could get the sentence in. Mrs. Williams said I ad-libbed and asked me where I learned to do that. I told her I didn't know. I just knew I had to think fast before I blew the lines, and they wouldn't make sense."

"That's great, son. I'm so proud of you." Mom replied. "All your hard work paid off."

"Yes, ma'am," Lennie answered. "Thanks for helping me."

That night, Lennie could hardly sleep for the excitement of seeing the cast list at school the following day.

When the teacher posted the cast list on her bulletin board, Lennie couldn't bear to look. Would he fail? Would his dream be shattered? His turn to look at the bulletin board arrived. Lennie placed his hand on the board and ran his finger over the list of cast members. Lead player: Lennie Stokes.

Lennie rushed home to tell his mother, glad he'd made the effort to try out. He had found something he was good at and loved it.

A man who doesn't try will never find success.

A COOP FULL OF CHICKENS

As a hen doth gather her brood under her wings.
—Luke 13:34 (KJV)

"Momma, look what Mrs. Young gave me," Cindy said as she ran into the kitchen.

"What in the world are you going to do with two chickens and a rooster?"

"I'm going to raise them, so you don't have to buy eggs."

"And how do you plan to do that? You don't know anything about chickens. They need a house and a pen so wild animals don't steal them. Besides, that rooster can't lay eggs."

"I didn't think about that, Momma. What good is he if he doesn't lay eggs?"

"A good rooster will protect the hens from predators, round them up when danger arises. Plus, he'll crow every morning to let you know it's time to get up and feed him. Your dad will have to help you build a pen and a coop for them. Get some of your birthday money from your room. Your dad will have to take you to buy some grain, fence, and building materials after supper."

"Okay, Mom. This can also be my school project. That'll be cool. I'll get fresh eggs and a good grade," Cindy said, then took her chickens outside.

"Lou Ann, did our neighbors get chickens today?" Dad asked when he got home from work. "I heard some when I got out of the truck. Sounded like they were close."

"Not the neighbors. The chickens are closer than you think. Your daughter can explain it to you."

"Oh no. Every time you say 'my daughter,' it winds up costing me." Dad grinned, then headed toward the tool shed. "Cindy, where are you? You've got some explaining to do, honey."

"Hey, Daddy," Cindy said as she shut the tool shed door.

"Why do I hear chickens?"

Cindy jumped into his arms and hugged him. "I'm gonna raise chickens. They're in the tool shed. Mom said we could go get some stuff for them after we eat."

"Go wash up for supper while I look at those birds."

While they ate Dad said, "Cindy, slow down before you choke. The farm store will be open when we get there."

When they finished eating, they hopped in the truck and went to town.

"Alright, girl. First, we'll need some chicken feed and a water dish. We'll get some boards and fence, but we can put the chickens in the garage until we build their pen this weekend."

With the pen and coop built, Cindy took her yard birds to their new home. The rooster started crowing while the hen scratched the ground for bugs. Dad threw out a couple of handfuls of grain.

"Chickens are a lot of work, aren't they, Dad?" she asked while he stood wiping sawdust and sweat from his face.

"And they're a lot of responsibility. Are you sure you can take care of them?"

"You better believe it, Dad. You'll see."

Cindy was right. She spent hours on the internet reading about chickens. By the end of the summer, Dad was selling fresh eggs to the guys at work, and Mom was baking cakes and cookies with Cindy's help to use the extra eggs. Her dad bought her four more chickens since she was taking care of the two so well. At twelve years old, Cindy learned to wield a hammer well putting up chicken wire. She could also gather eggs without the chickens pecking her.

Weeks later, Cindy ran into the house and yelled for her mom. "Somebody gave me some more chickens. They weren't there this morning when I fed them. There are four more, but they're little bitty."

Mom laughed. "No one gave you those chicks. They hatched from the eggs that Momma hen wouldn't let you get. She wasn't being mean like you thought. She just knew her babies were due to hatch any day. That's the other thing the rooster is for. He's the daddy of those chicks. When they get older, they'll start laying eggs too."

"Can I hold the chicks, Momma?" Cindy beamed with excitement.

"Slowly try to pick one up. If the hen doesn't peck you, it'll be alright. I'm proud of you, Cindy. I knew you could do it if you tried hard enough, and you got an A on your project. A few months from now, you'll have more eggs than you can keep up with."

Where there's a will, there's a way.

CHOMPIN' AT THE BIT

David hasted and ran toward the army to meet the
Philistine.
—1 Samuel 17:48 (KJV)

"Son, settle down. And don't forget to brush your teeth. I've told you four times already," Mom said with a slight hint of frustration. On Clint's first day of preschool, he was wound as tight as a banjo string.

"I did, Mom," Clint said, flying past her and toward the door.

"Clinton Douglas Smith, where are your shoes? Get back in here. I know you're excited, but you can't go to preschool without shoes."

"Yes, Momma. I can't wait to play with the other kids."

"You've got two years of preschool, thirteen years till graduation, and several years of college or trade school. No use being in such a hurry. Here are your shoes. Sit down and put them on the right feet," Mom said, shaking her head and turning to hide a laugh.

What could she say to an excited three-year-old to calm him down? Nothing. All she could do as a parent was hope he maintained that enthusiasm all his educational years. She looked forward to seeing him make friends, learn to play well with others, and discover the wonder of learning.

Fast-forward twenty-some years. The young man with all the various-colored tassels is Mom's little boy, Clint. He's all grown up and ready to step out into a big world that's waiting to chew him up and spit him out. She keeps telling herself not to worry because Clint has kept that spark of excitement for learning.

Mom and Dad couldn't be prouder as Clint prepares to deliver his commencement speech. In a little while, he'll flip his tassel to the other side of his graduation cap and leave college with his degree in commercial architecture. His whole life has been spent pouring his heart and soul into everything he has ever done. His new job in Chicago will be his first challenge in the real world.

A couple of hours later, Mom watches with a mile-wide grin and watery eyes as Clint walks across the stage. It seems like only yesterday he was an excited little boy running out without his shoes, going to preschool. In nine days, he'll load his pickup and move to Chicago. But right now, as he throws his arms around her, she savors those sweet memories of yesteryear.

"Clint, your dad, and I are so proud of you! You've been chompin' at the bit all your life in everything you've done. Welcome to the real world, son. You'll always be my baby, and I'll miss you, but you'll do fine," Mom said, wiping away tears of joy.

"Thanks, Mom, I could've never done it without you and Dad always believing in me. All I've ever wanted was to make you proud and never disappoint you."

"We've always been proud. You've always been an obedient son, and we've never been disappointed in you.

"Thanks, Mom. I've got to run to get home and pack my stuff. I'll see you at home."

"What do you mean, get your stuff together? You still have a week and a half before you leave."

"I know, but I might go a few days early. Do some sightseeing or maybe report to work early."

"OK, son. See you in a little while. You're still the same old Clint. Chompin' at the bit. Always in a hurry to start something new." Mom hugged him again, then kissed him goodbye before he got in his truck and drove away.

Always face your challenges head-on with enthusiasm.

KEEP POUNDING THE ROCK

*I can do all things through Christ which
strengtheneth me.*
—Philippians 4:13 (KJV)

"You'll never move that rock, Mikey. It's too big." Not very encouraging, but Mikey had grown used to hearing that from his friends. Ever since his family had moved to their home when he was three years old, Mikey had hated that rock. He wanted his dad to move it to make room for a swing set, and his dad promised to buy one if he moved the rock.

Only six when his dad made that promise, Mikey spent every day trying to move that rock. Sometimes he tried only a few times when he went outside to play. On other days, Mikey tried for hours. He first started with the hammer in the tool kit he got for Christmas. When that didn't work, he used his dad's hammer. Still unsuccessful, Mikey saved his birthday money and bought a three-pound sledgehammer. With a boatload of determination that some might call a stubborn streak, he kept trying to move that rock.

As he entered his teen years, Mikey accepted the fact that rock would probably always be there. Nevertheless, he didn't give up. By age fourteen, Mikey had bought a ten-pound sledgehammer. When he made the varsity football team, primarily because of his size and strength, he decided that rock could be helpful in his training regimen.

Each day, Mikey spent an hour jumping on the top of the rock and pounding it thirty licks with his hammer. He then jumped down and back up again and did another thirty. He had long since forgotten about the swing set.

On signing day of his senior year, he signed a scholarship letter of intent for a full ride to one of the most prominent football universities in the South. At supper, he asked his dad, "Are you ever going to move that rock?"

"Why should I? Look what it did for you?"

"What do you mean, Dad?"

"Mikey, since you were six, you've tried to move that rock. You worked at it every day, even breaking a few hammers along the way. That rock never moved, but it did something for you I never could've. That rock made you strong. Although you hated it, it's the reason you're where you are today. If not for that rock, you would've spent your time playing video games or doing something else. Instead, you're about to live out your dream of playing college ball. Your hard work, determination, and perseverance got you here. I'm proud of you, son."

Mikey realized that the obstacle that hindered him the most molded him into what he strived to become. Our trials help us develop compassion for others going through them. They create in us a desire to alleviate someone else's suffering. They motivate us to encourage others in their struggles. Those situations we hate and don't think we'll ever survive make us who we are. As the years passed, Mikey told many others the story of the rock and always added, "Keep pounding the rocks in your life."

What doesn't kill us only makes us stronger.

MAJOR GENERAL SMULEY RUFUS

My little children, let us not love in word,
neither in tongue, but in deed and in truth.
—1 John 3:18 (KJV)

"Smuley, you're the most stubborn, muleheaded youngin' I've ever seen!" yelled his mom as he ran through the yard. And so the nickname of Mrs. Rufus's youngest boy was born. With a name like Armond, he didn't think Smuley (stubborn mule) was all that bad.

Smuley Rufus was a likable kid but easily bored and impulsive, which sometimes led to trouble. At seventeen, he left the red clay roads of Alabama to join the Marines, just like his dad. Mr. Rufus, a proud leatherneck, had died in a plane crash. Smuley's mom thought the discipline would do him good, so she signed the permission papers for him to enlist early.

His neighbors and friends were surprised when Smuley became a highly respected Marine and rose quickly through the ranks. He served proudly in the Gulf War and earned his stripes as a drill instructor. Folks back home were amazed that this hyper, impulsive, rambunctious boy was now a career officer in the military. He fooled a lot of folks who figured he'd never amount to anything. Or wind up in jail. Or dead. But his mom was right. The discipline and challenges of Marine life were what Smuley needed all along.

Smuley's most rewarding battle came after seventeen years of service. One of his recruits was accused of starting a brawl while on leave.

"Private Connie Braxton. What kind of a name is Connie for a Marine, son? Is it short for Conrad?" Smuley asked.

"Yes, sir."

"My mom said I was stubborn and muleheaded. She combined both words into Smuley, and it stuck. What can I do for you, soldier?"

"Sir, I'm accused of starting a brawl while on leave. My trial is in two weeks. I could be kicked out of the Corps on an assault charge. Sir, I enlisted to pay my little sister's way through nursing school. Besides, being a Marine is all I've ever wanted to do, sir."

"What happened?"

"An Army guy was harassing a young lady in a restaurant. When she tried to leave, he grabbed her arm. I told him to let her go. He released her arm and took a swing at me. I ducked and turned to walk her out, but he jumped me from behind. I fought back to defend myself."

"Okay, son. Send me your court date and time. Dress right and be there early."

"Yes, sir. Thanks again, sir," Connie said with a sharp salute.

Smuley was in the gallery when Connie arrived in court. He and the girl at the center of the incident took the stand in Connie's defense. The charges were dropped.

Eighteen years later, on a bright summer day, a retirement ceremony was held honoring Smuley for his thirty-five-year career.

The guest of honor was now a two-star Major General.

While Smuley mingles with the guests, he heard a voice behind him.

"Major General, sir."

He turned to see a short, stocky officer in his mid-thirties saluting him.

As Smuley returned the salute, the young man said, "Sir, you don't remember me, do you?"

"No, Colonel, I'm afraid I don't."

"Colonel Connie Braxton, sir. Thank you for believing in me when I was in trouble as a recruit. I wish you the best in your retirement."

"Braxton. I remember now. You were paying for your sister to attend nursing school. I'm glad you stuck it out. Did your sister get through school?"

"Yes, sir," Connie replied. "She joined the Corps and is now the head nurse at the base hospital. Thank you again. I hope I've made you proud, sir."

"Without question, Colonel. You've also made my day. Here's my card. If you ever get down to Alabama, call me up. We'll break bread and talk about the Corps. By the way, what happened to that young lady you defended?"

"I married her, sir. And I'd like very much to visit you in Alabama." Connie saluted again and walked away.

"Bring your family, soldier," Smuley yelled as Connie disappeared into the crowd.

Over his thirty-five-year career, many officers believed in Smuley.

He believed in Colonel Connie Braxton, just like many people in his career once believed in him.

Your belief in someone can help determine the course of their life.

OVERCOMING ADVERSITY— NEVER GIVE UP

Seven modern parables of people who never gave up.

"Don't Quit" is the title of a poem written by British-born American poet Edgar A. Guest. An optimistic person, Guest used his talent for writing to encourage others. No one is immune to trouble or difficult circumstances in life. I often read the poem when adversity becomes a constant companion.

Down home in western North Carolina, we face years of recovery following Hurricane Helene. It would be easy to throw up our hands and quit when we look at the destruction of the areas where we grew up and hear the numerous survival stories. What's even worse is the stories of those who perished in the storm. But, as I've known all my life, mountain people are resilient. Faith and family are the top priorities of most who've grown up here. Life is much different than when I was a kid, but the one constant is a love of God and family.

Sometimes adversity hangs like a weight around one's neck. In those times, we must reach deep inside ourselves to find the will to keep going. You never fail until you quit trying. Each of us must decide how we will handle adversity. Will we allow it to make us better or make us bitter against life and the Lord?

Joseph's story in Scripture is a great example of overcoming adversity. His brothers became jealous of him and his special place in his dad's heart. Angry about a dream he shared with them about one day ruling over them, they cast him into a pit and sold him into slavery to passing merchants. Little did his brothers know they had started the wheels turning for his dream to come true.

Joseph was sold again on the auction block and purchased by Potiphar, a high officer in Pharaoh's court. Potiphar's wife tried to seduce Joseph, then lied about him when he refused. He was imprisoned, then later forgotten by two prisoners, a butler and a baker, whose dreams he had interpreted.

After his reinstatement to the palace, the butler remembered Joseph when Pharaoh needed a dream interpreted. Joseph appeared before the king, explained his dream, and was released and promoted. He rose to be the second most powerful man in the kingdom. When a drought hit, Joseph oversaw all the gathering and dispersal of grain in Egypt and held that position when his brothers came to Egypt to buy food. They bowed to him without recognizing him, but he eventually revealed himself to them and was able to preserve his entire family and move them to Egypt at Pharaoh's command. He went from the pit to Potiphar's household to the prison and finally to the second most powerful position in Pharaoh's palace. Joseph knew firsthand about a life filled with overcoming adversity.

The stories in this section demonstrate how even in the darkest situations, God can come through when we least expect Him to. When we don't even think He's listening, He's already working on our problem. Just as fruit must mature before being harvested, situations we face must play out before God can accomplish His purpose by solving them. Instant answers and solutions don't create the faith and confidence to face future circumstances with grace and dignity or give us a closer walk with God.

Sometimes our adversity isn't self-inflicted. Unforeseen circumstances, such as in Joseph's case, may trap us in adversity for years. Even when the outcome isn't due to bad decisions, it may affect us long-term. Others around us can also be affected, which often creates internal conflict. We wonder if we could've done anything differently. At the end of the day, though, we're still left with adversity, even when it's beyond our control.

Applying yourself to everything you do is vital. Set goals that some may think are too lofty and seemingly unattainable, and then apply yourself to reaching them. You may encounter adversity even though your goals are admirable. The reward is the eventual satisfaction of attaining your goals despite the disbelief of others or the difficulty of your journey. The main thing is never to give up. You'll find that maximum effort, perseverance, prayer, and dedication are the keys to overcoming adversity.

DOWN, BUT NOT OUT

*Inasmuch as ye have done it unto one of the least of
these, my brethren, ye have done it unto me.*
—Matthew 25:40 (KJV)

Cassie's story would break even the toughest hearts. Her husband, Bud, had been severely injured in a car accident. With three kids and one on the way, times were desperate, and her pride was out the window. She took help wherever she could get it. Today was just like yesterday, and tomorrow looked like more of the same.

Terry was a local mechanic with a good reputation for honesty and quality work. He lived comfortably but not extravagantly. Having raised a couple of daughters of his own and now having several grandchildren, he remembered how hard it was sometimes to stretch a dollar past the breaking point. He had worked jobs no one else wanted. He had cut and sold wood on evenings and weekends to make ends meet. Although he never let his family do without, he gave away a few pickup loads when he saw someone in need. If helping someone ran him a little short on cash, he worked more hours the next week.

As it would have been divine providence, Cassie met someone who referred her to Terry for mechanical work. Not one to say no and being a sucker for kids, Terry agreed to work on her car. The bald tires were the least of his concerns. The missing muffler and the likelihood of carbon monoxide getting to those young'uns in the back seat were more than he could stand. Even though she hadn't asked for it, he replaced the muffler. The spark plugs looked like they had been through a fire. The plug wires were no better. After all the engine problems were fixed, the car ran like a Swiss watch. Terry then turned his attention to those tires. Going through his leftover parts, he found four that were the right size. They weren't new, but at least no cords were showing through the rubber.

After taking it through the car wash, Terry called Cassie and told her the car was ready. She got off the city bus in front of Terry's house, worried if she had enough money. Terry walked up the driveway from his garage with a smile.

"You look tired," he said.

"I don't mind riding the bus, but it takes forever to get across town," she replied. "How much do I owe you?"

"Start it up first and see if it sounds okay to you."

Turning the key, she noticed the engine light that had been on for months was finally out.

"My light is out!" she said.

"Nothing new plugs and wires couldn't fix. Your inspection was due, so I did that too. Does seventy-five dollars sound fair to you?" Terry asked.

"Are you serious?" Cassie replied. "I was expecting twice that much."

Terry didn't mention the other parts he replaced.

She dug in her purse and pulled out some wadded-up bills.

"Hang on," she said. "That's just seventy. I've got a five in here somewhere."

"Close enough," Terry said. "I'm glad you're happy. At least now you won't have to worry about those young'uns riding around on bald tires."

"My car hasn't sounded this good since I've owned it. Don't ever remember it looking this good either," Cassie said as the engine purred like a kitten lapping up a bowl of milk.

"Maybe you can take that five and pick up a carton of ice cream for your kids on the way home," Terry suggested.

"Good idea. They don't get special treats often. I can't thank you enough, Terry. I heard you would do me right, but I never expected this."

"Just take care of those young'uns and let me know if you have any more problems," Terry said as she backed into the road.

"I will," she replied. "God bless you."

"He already has. Far more than I deserve."

Later that evening, after supper, his wife looked at the receipts. "You didn't charge her for all the parts or the labor. That was nice of you."

Terry reached over and took his wife's hand. "I remember a young couple who used to be where she is now. Everyone needs a little help sometimes."

Never forget where you came from.

WHEN THE GOING GETS TOUGH

And Moses was an hundred and twenty years old when he died: his eye was not dim, nor his natural force abated.
—Deuteronomy 34:7 (KJV)

Hubert was too old to work and too poor to quit. He had spent his life trucking, but life in the freight business is physically and mentally demanding. He learned to deal with the mental stuff, but the physical was a different story. Old body parts wear out.

That's where Hubert found himself. Too old to keep up the pace. At sixty-eight years old, he was being forced out. His mind was still sharp, but his body was sore and slowing down. Some of the young guys called him Grandpa or Old Man. Hubert didn't mind. But when they said, "Grandpa, you're too old for this. Why don't you hang it up?"—that got under his skin.

Even though Hubert's wife had been in heaven for two years, he was still paying the nursing home bill from his wife's stay there. He had grown up in a time when you didn't shirk responsibility, and you always kept your word. One of the sayings he lived by was "When the going gets tough, the tough get going."

Now, his bosses were telling him to get going.

They were right. He was getting too old. Each day it was tougher to load and unload his rig.

But trucking was all he knew, so he cashed out some of his retirement and bought himself a truck. He hired a twenty-four-year-old man at church with a wife and three kids. Hubert had been about that age when he started trucking. He taught the young man to drive and helped him get his Class A Commercial Driver's License.

Hubert became a grandpa to young Larry's family. Larry's wife even invited him to supper every night. Larry was a good worker, and it wasn't long before Hubert saved enough money to buy another truck. When he paid off the nursing home bill, he slowly turned the reins over to Larry to run the business. Four trucks later, Hubert signed his company over to Larry, lock, stock, and barrel.

Those young guys at his old company were proven wrong. Hubert wasn't too old to work. He couldn't do the work he once did, but he still had a good mind and determination. A little older and wiser, those boys saw the error of their ways. Hubert even hired some of them before he retired and taught them how to be resilient and never give up.

Hubert had also proven he was one tough old bull who wasn't ready to be put out to pasture.

When the going gets tough, the tough get going.

MORE THAN YOU CAN CHEW

If ye then, being evil, Father, know how to give good
gifts unto your children, how much more shall your
Father, which is in heaven give good things to them
that ask him?
—Matthew 7:11 (KJV)

No matter how hard he tried, Travis couldn't throw a curveball. He practiced daily, but he couldn't do it. His parents encouraged him, "Always do your best." Travis loved baseball, but his athletic skills were poor. Still, the team camaraderie and hanging out with his friends appealed to him and made the game fun.

His best efforts didn't measure up, but he loved to play. Everyone else was bigger, but Travis had heart. Despite his shortcomings, he showed up to every practice.

As he got older, he turned to music, did pretty well, and loved it. Yet again, he was mediocre at best. His coordination and sense of timing were always a bit off. He heard all the usual encouragements. "Always going to be someone a little better than you, but do your best" was a common saying, but brought little comfort. Doing his best didn't seem to improve his skill level.

Barely more than five feet nothing and a little pudgy, the only thing Travis excelled at was mediocrity. When he finally accepted that he didn't have to be the best at everything, he became pretty good in several areas—science, math, and landscaping, to name a few. He lived some of his dreams, enjoyed life, always loved people, and spent his life volunteering and giving to others.

Travis received an award for having the most hours of community service in his high school. The director insisted that he give a speech at their annual volunteer banquet. With his usual humility, Travis stepped to the podium, cleared his throat, and said, "I've never accomplished all I've wanted to. I realize that sometimes I've bitten off more than I could chew. From those experiences, I've learned that we may not all have the gifts and abilities we'd like. God gives people different gifts to accomplish his purpose in our lives. It's not always that something is more than we can chew; often, we're just chewing on the wrong things. Thank you all for this award. It has been my honor to help my community and my school."

Don't bite off more than you can chew.

GET RIGHT BACK ON

And said to his servant, Go up now, look toward the
sea. And he went up, and looked, and said, There is
nothing. And he said, Go again seven times.
—1 Kings 18:43 (KJV)

Ricky was learning how to ride his new bicycle. Thank God for the training wheels that helped him keep his balance. He could hardly wait for his dad to get home from work to help him practice while Mom cooked dinner.

Dad grabbed a wrench from the garage and began removing the training wheels. Ricky objected, but it was no use. Dad's mind was made up. The time had come for Ricky to learn to ride like his brother and his friends. Ricky got on the bike, and Dad rolled him out to the little hill where his brother Roger had learned to ride. Dad ran alongside Ricky until he couldn't keep up anymore.

"Dad! It's going too fast. I'm going to wreck," Ricky cried out as he headed toward the ditch.

"Hang on and watch where you're going," Dad hollered as he tried to catch up. "Lightly squeeze your back brake handle."

That did nothing to alleviate Ricky's fears as the bike gained speed. Finally, the inevitable happened. As he hit the bottom of the dip, Ricky rolled off the road uphill into the grass and fell over. More scared than hurt, he began to cry.

His dad ran to check on him. "That was incredible, son!" he said as he bent over to pick up Ricky off the ground.

"But Dad, I crashed my new bike. I want my training wheels back." He wiped away tears as he sobbed.

"You don't need training wheels! Look how far you rode. Everyone wrecks when they're first learning to ride. I'm so proud of you, son!"

Dad picked up the bike and started rolling it up the hill. Ricky was still sniffling when he turned to his dad and asked, "Why are you proud, Dad? Mom's gonna be mad when she sees my new britches with grass stains on them."

Ricky's dad was sure he could calm Mom about the grass stains. When she saw Ricky rubbing his eyes, she would be more concerned with him than his britches. Dad said, "She'll be proud of you too. Just wait until I tell her how good you did. She might even fix peach cobbler with ice cream for dessert to celebrate." Dad tussled Ricky's hair and put his ball cap back on his head. "Come on, let's try it again. We won't go all the way up this time."

"Oh no," Ricky replied as he tried to quit sniffling. "I'm never riding again. I don't like bicycles anymore. I'll walk everywhere I go." He started back up the hill.

Dad had heard the same complaints a few years earlier when he taught Roger how to ride.

"Roger never wrecks. I wish I could ride as good as him. I'm done. I don't like it anymore."

"He crashed worse than you on his first ride without training wheels. I had to straighten his handlebars because he bent them so badly. Roger cried and stomped off just like you, swearing he'd never ride again. But later, he decided he'd learn no matter what it took. He practiced every day. He wrecked a lot but kept getting back on every time. Now, he can even ride a wheelie on the back tire."

"I'll never be that good, Dad," Ricky said, wiping the last tears.

"Sure you will, son. It just takes a lot of practice. You won't always get everything right the first time you do it. You'll mess up sometimes for the rest of your life, no matter what you do. The secret is when you fall in the dirt, pick yourself up, get right back on, and try again. Here, get your bike. Are you ready to go again?"

"Yes, sir, Dad," Ricky said and grabbed the handlebars.

Life is like learning to ride a bicycle.
No matter how many times you fall in the dirt,
get up, and get right back on.

STILL WORTH SOWING

Commit thy works unto the LORD,
and thy thoughts shall be established.
—Proverbs 16:3 (KJV)

Jess watched as his dad turned the old red tractor at the end of the garden. Each year, it was the same story. Plow, disk, till, and plant. The farm life wasn't easy, and Jess wasn't sure he wanted to follow in Dad's footsteps. The windstorms last summer had blown down about half of the corn, then two straight weeks of rain had drowned many of the beans. They had a decent harvest, but many of the bean plants rotted in the field weeks before the harvest.

The story was the same with pretty much the whole garden. Why did his dad keep doing the same thing over and over, expecting a different result? The monotonous routine seemed pointless to Jess.

Dad finally pulled the old tractor to a stop under a big apple tree near the garden. As they ate lunch, Jess figured his dad had to have a rational reason for doing all the planting, only to lose a lot of it to weather beyond his control. A lot of what didn't blow down or drown got baked by the hot midwestern sun.

"Dad, why do you plant so much and work so hard, knowing you always lose a lot of it? Fuel and fertilizer are expensive, yet you continue to spend on them. Seems like a waste. Why not trade with livestock and quit all the planting?"

"Well, son, it's like this," Dad said, pushing back his hat and wiping the sweat from his forehead. "The livestock eat the silage from the corn that survives till harvest. We get seeds from the bean plants that survive, and many that don't make it still have good seeds. The entire garden is the same way. I plant a lot, knowing not all of it will come up. But what survives until harvest will provide food for the animals and for us until next year."

"That kind of makes sense, but why not get a job in town?" Jess asked as Dad unscrewed the lid on his jug of iced tea.

"Farming is more than just dirt and crops and harvests. It's a way of life. I've never done anything else and haven't wanted to. It gets in your blood, and even if it kills you, you'll die doing what you love. Even with the losses, we always have enough for our family, the stock, and plenty for your mom to can and give to others. We even sell some at the farmers' market. It's a simple answer, son." Dad pushed his hat back and wiped dirty sweat from his face. "You don't worry about the stuff you can't do anything about. Only sixty percent of our crops may survive till harvest in a bad year. Although not all our seeds may produce, we continue planting because some do," Dad said and climbed back on the tractor. "It isn't about what you lose but what you gain."

"I hadn't thought about it like that, Dad. Do you really love it that much?"

"It's a lot of work, but where else can you stay outside all day enjoying the sun and rain? Plus, where else can you see a cow, goat, or pig bring babies into the world or ride horses or lay back on fresh-cut hay when you get tired? One more thing that I really like."

"What's that, Dad?"

"During the summer, I get to bring my kid to work with me and spend quality moments like this, just talking."

"I guess it's not so bad after all, since you put it like that," Jess said as he cleaned some mud from the tractor wheels. "Not bad at all."

Don't worry about the stuff you can't do anything about.

OLD WORKBOOTS

And if thou draw out thy soul to the hungry,
and satisfy the afflicted soul; then shall thy light rise
in obscurity, and thy darkness be as the noonday.
—Isaiah 58:10 (KJV)

Bobby had worn a bare spot in the grass where he stood holding his sign asking for handouts. He didn't know it yet, but when an old red pickup slowed to a stop that Saturday morning, his life and luck were about to change forever.

With their first handshake, a beautiful and enduring friendship began between the driver and his passenger. "Are you willing to grab a bite to eat and talk about some work?" Franklin said after introducing himself. "You're serious about working, aren't you?"

"Yes, sir. I sure am." Bobby straightened his shoulders and brushed his hair back. He climbed into the truck, and the two headed to a diner down the street.

"Tell me a little about yourself. I don't remember seeing you out here till recently." Franklin flipped on his turn signal and pulled into traffic.

"Not much to tell, sir. I had a good job but lost it and my truck when the plant closed. Now I take any work I can get and stand on the corner collecting change."

"Must be tough being homeless."

"Oh, I'm not homeless. I have a wife and two little girls. We're living in an old trailer until we get back on our feet. Carol's a full-time mom," Bobby said.

"Here we are," Franklin said as he pulled into the gravel parking lot. "This place has the best gravy in town. Order what you want. They've got anything you could want for breakfast."

"Franklin, I swear you terrorize me enough when you come in by yourself," Kayla said as she placed the silverware on the table. "Now, you've brought back-up. What can I get for you?"

"This here's Bobby. My stomach's already gnawing on my backbone. Give me the big sawmill gravy and scrambled eggs platter to start with."

"Nice to meet you, Bobby. You gotta watch Franklin. Don't let him get you in any trouble," Kayla said with a smile. "What'll you have?"

"Give me the same as him, and add a waffle and hashbrowns on the side."

"Don't you let him make you pay for his breakfast. He's a slick one. I told you you've got to watch him." She grabbed the coffee pot and poured them each a cup.

The men worked all day Saturday and made plans to begin again the following weekend. When Franklin took Bobby home, he noticed the younger man's boots—ragged and held together with duct tape. "Those boots have seen better days. What size are they? About a ten?" Franklin asked.

"Nine."

On Monday evening, Franklin stopped at Bobby's intersection. "Come on, Bobby. Let's go eat."

"Sure thing, thanks." Bobby hopped into the truck. As they neared the diner, Franklin slowed to turn into the parking lot.

"Open that box there on the floor. See what you think of them. I got them from the shoe truck at work today."

"Those are sharp," Bobby replied.

"Put 'em on," Franklin said.

"Are you serious?"

"As hard as you work, you're worth much more than a pair of boots. Didn't come with duct tape, but I hope you don't mind." A grin stretched across Franklin's face as he opened the car door.

A man's value is not measured by his possessions
but by his willingness to do his best.

AIM HIGH

*Be ye strong, therefore, and let not your hands be
weak: for your work shall be rewarded.*
—2 Chronicles 15:7 (KJV)

Jason had worked at the airport since he was sixteen. Now, at twenty-four, with a wife and a new baby, he needed something more lucrative. The pay was decent for a man with a high school diploma, but the hours fluctuated from twenty to sixty or more at the height of the tourist season. With a stack of hospital bills and no insurance, Jason needed a full-time job with benefits. He hated the thought of leaving the airport, but how could he move up from maintenance without more education?

As he cleaned up for the evening, he noticed a job posted on the bulletin board:

Wanted

Full-time maintenance technician for hangar and airport grounds
Apply to Human Resources

This full-time position offered potential for advancement and special training, but it required a two-year college degree, which Jason didn't have.

"Hey Jason, I've been looking all over for you," his friend Dale called out to him as he came in the door. "I hope you don't mind, but I put in your name for the job opening in the hangar."

"I appreciate it, but you know I don't have a degree."

"You've worked here since high school, and everyone knows what a hard worker you are. They might even send you to school to become an aircraft mechanic. Mr. Mitchell is retiring in three years, and they'll have to replace him." Dale shoved his hands into his pockets. "If you apply and are willing to work the day shift and take a few evening classes, they might hire you. You'd work with Mr. Mitchell and get on-the-job training at the same time. I told them I was sure you'd apply and that you fit the bill."

"I'll think about it."

"Don't think about it. You need a job, and they need a body. And you have experience."

"Alright, already. I'll talk to HR tomorrow during my lunch break."

Three weeks later, Jason started his new position as a hangar maintenance technician and apprentice mechanic. His benefits included tuition and books for his courses at the community college. All he had to do was graduate.

At the end of two years, Jason walked across the stage to receive his diploma. With the golden tassel brushing against his neck, he proved to himself what everyone else already knew. He was ambitious, applied himself, finished at the top of his class, and graduated with high honors.

Those who believed in him were in the front row, cheering louder than anyone else. Jason smiled as he shook the college president's hand. He'd taken the chance and succeeded.

Aim high.
You never know how high you will fly.

HONESTY

Seven stories that emphasize the unwavering value of honesty.

Famous Presbyterian evangelist and professional baseball player Billy Sunday once said, "An excuse is the skin of a reason stuffed with a lie."

"It was just a little white lie." There's no such thing. When Peter denied Christ in the courtyard of Pilate's Hall, he preceded his denial with two lies followed by a tirade of cursing. The gospel he had preached and his loyalty to Christ for over three years were—with only three comments—called into question, and a shroud of doubt was cast over his ministry. After repenting, Peter was appointed by Christ to "strengthen the brethren" (Luke 22:32 KJV). He also became one of the first evangelists to the gentiles. You can redeem yourself over time in the sight of most people, but some will never forget your past.

"No one will ever know." God will. The problem with dishonesty is that you always wonder who knows and if they'll say anything. The truth will come out at the most inconvenient time and place. Dishonesty may serve you well in the short term, but it will cost you dearly when exposed. No one wants dishonest friends—they can't be trusted, and their promises can't be relied on. One of the most common traits of an honest person is integrity, which describes someone who has strong moral principles and is upright in their dealings with others.

Who doesn't like to be around people of that caliber? Their personality traits draw people to them.

Honesty isn't always easy, but it's always right. The following stories highlight some of the pitfalls of dishonesty. Sometimes honesty may keep you from acquiring things or positions you might want. There are times when someone can keep quiet and not reveal facts known to be true. While that itself isn't dishonest, when the facts come to light, depending on the situation, it calls into question the character or integrity of the person withholding them.

Another adage says, "Let your conscience be your guide." That can end well for the type of honest person in the stories you're about to read. But if a person doesn't adhere to honesty and a moral code of ethics, their corrupted conscience will guide them to wrong decisions. When it comes to dishonest folks, some say, "They wouldn't know the truth if it walked up and bit them." That kind of character and reputation doesn't garner respect from anyone. It has the opposite effect, leading people to conclude that the person can't be trusted.

Conscience is the personal indicator or moral compass that determines our actions. It's the strong feeling or inner voice that guides us. For Christians, Christ is the moral compass in our lives. His Holy Spirit speaks to us through prayer, pointing out when we've done wrong, been deceitful, or even misleading. Those who are deceitful never have a clear conscience; they're always looking over their shoulder. Half-truths are a copout. They're still dishonest or misleading. If we aren't careful, we'll use them to soothe our conscience and justify inappropriate actions and behaviors.

Even though the truth can sometimes be hurtful, it's usually well-received and appreciated when communicated with love and compassion. I hope you enjoy the following stories and can see the importance of being honest. Romans 12:17 commands us to "provide things honest in the sight of all men" (KJV). Proverbs 22:1 says, "A good name is rather to be chosen than great riches, and loving favour rather than silver and gold" (KJV).

To acquire "a good name," you must be honest. Your record of being truthful will build a reputation for honesty. Being honest with others begins with being honest with yourself. Most of all, be honest with God. He will judge everyone in heaven with His word. Honesty shouldn't just be a character trait. It should be a way of life.

THE MOMENT OF TRUTH

In all thy ways acknowledge him, and he shall direct
thy paths.
—Proverbs 3:6 (KJV)

Alex was down to crunch time for his SAT (Scholastic Aptitude Test) and feared he wouldn't pass. Having excellent grades, he planned to apply to Duke University in Durham, NC, for pre-med.

One night while studying at the kitchen table, Alex heard a knock at the front door. He rubbed his eyes and stood, then ran to look through the peephole. No one. One o'clock in the morning, and some jerk was playing jokes on him. Another knock. Again, no one there. Alex ran out the door and, tripping over a backpack, nearly face-planted on the porch. Since it was so late, he'd try to find the backpack's owner in the morning and return it.

Choking down a pastry before going to school, Alex grabbed his backpack. As he reached to close the front door, he saw the other one. There was no identification, but a folder inside was labeled SAT. It contained a complete set of answers for his upcoming test. Alex stored the backpack in his room until he decided what to do with it. Cheating wasn't right, but he could use the help. A high SAT score, his high school transcript, and hopefully finishing third in his class would assure him a spot at Duke.

Alex was raised to be honest, and he knew cheating wouldn't please

God or his parents. He took the backpack and the folder to the SAT administrators and explained that someone left them at his door. They thanked him for his honesty. He felt a sense of relief, yet also a sense of dread about the test.

Weeks later, his test results came in the mail. He hadn't done as well as he'd hoped. Disappointed, he became nervous when a Duke University envelope arrived in the mail. Just as he'd feared, Duke wasn't looking for above average. They were looking for excellence.

If God closes one door, he always opens a better one. He'd rely on his faith and wait to see what the Lord would do. Three days later, a letter came from NC State. They had requested his transcript from his STEM (science, technology, engineering, and math) high school. They were beginning a water-system engineering and design program intended to bring fresh water to villages in third world countries. They were particularly interested in his transcript because he excelled at all forms of math and science, and they offered him a scholarship to enroll in that program.

Alex realized his goals and God's plan were quite different. The offer meant a free education, so he enrolled. He didn't sell out his integrity or faith to buy his dreams.

Upon graduation, Alex was offered a job where he'd get to see the world and help people in ways doctors never could. His employer designed water systems. His first assignment was designing a water system in a poor village on a mountain in Honduras.

Several years later, Alex watches women go to the well he designed and installed. They no longer hike through the jungle a half mile for water they boil before using. These women and children are now healthy because of the fresh water he brought to their village.

Alex hears a knock at his door and opens it. A small woman stands there with two children and a basket of vegetables—a gift to thank him for the water she uses to grow the garden that feeds her family and helps lift them from poverty through the sale of the produce. He relishes the satisfaction of making people healthy and rescuing them from desperation.

When the woman hugs him and turns to leave, he realizes that God opened a much better door when he trusted Him in his moment of truth and did the right thing.

Honesty is the best policy.

BE AS GOOD AS YOUR WORD

Fathers, provoke not your children to anger,
lest they be discouraged.
—Colossians 3:21 (KJV)

Teddy was out of bed before daylight, so excited he couldn't sleep. His dad had promised to take him on his first fishing trip today. Judging by everything he wanted to take, one would think it would be a week-long expedition, not a day trip.

"Momma, where could Daddy be? He promised he'd be here." Teddy stood in the driveway, tears streaming down his face. "I've got my fishing pole and everything, Mom. He promised."

"I know, son." Mom bent down to hug him. "Something must have come up. I'll call and see what's delaying him."

Teddy's mom and dad had separated in January. Now, she was a single mom raising a six-year-old on her own. Although she and Teddy's father had their differences, she knew he would never do anything to disappoint his son.

"What time is it, Mom?

"Five minutes till seven. Why?"

"When Dad called Monday, he told me to be waiting in the driveway at 7:00 a.m. sharp. Why would Dad forget about me, Mom?"

"Your dad would never forget you," she said, trying to sound reassuring. "Maybe his truck broke down. It is pretty old and beat up."

Just as he was about to go back inside, Teddy heard the rumble of Dad's old truck as he turned onto their street.

"Momma, Momma, he did come!" Teddy's face transformed from a teary frown to an elated smile. When his dad stopped the truck, Teddy ran to meet him.

"How's Daddy's little man?" Dad bent down to catch Teddy jumping into his arms. "Sorry, I'm almost late, son. I had to stop for gas."

"I thought you forgot about me," he said as Dad wiped the tears from his face.

"I could never forget you, buddy. Besides, this is our first fishing trip together. I wouldn't miss that for the world. Let's grab your gear and put it in the truck. We'll stop by the diner for a quick breakfast. We don't want to keep those fish waiting. They might decide they're not hungry after all." Dad settled Teddy in the booster seat and put his pole and tackle box in the truck bed.

"Sorry, I cut it so close, Sheila. I hope he wasn't too much of a handful."

"He's been a handful since you called Monday, Walt. It would've been a long week trying to mend his broken little heart if you hadn't come. Y'all have fun and be careful."

"We will. See you tonight." Walt got into the truck to back out of the driveway.

"Bye, Momma. I'm gonna catch a big one for supper just like Dad does. Love you."

"Love you too, son. Mind your dad."

Teddy waved to her with a grin so big it looked like it would swallow his ears.

A person should always be as good as their word.

SCOUT'S HONOR

*He that hath pity upon the poor lendeth unto the
LORD; and that which he hath given will he pay him
again.*
—Proverbs 19:17 (KJV)

Jeremy, a decorated Boy Scout, loved scouting. His neighbor, Ivan Jones, was a retired and disabled veteran of Operation Desert Storm. Jeremy often helped Mr. Jones with chores. One Friday morning, Mr. Jones called him before he went to school.

"Jeremy, could you come to my house after school today?"

"Sure thing, Mr. Jones. I'll see you this afternoon," Jeremy replied before he hung up the phone.

When Jeremy got home, he went straight to his neighbor's house. In the yard, someone had delivered a load of firewood.

"Hello, Jeremy. How was school?" Mr. Jones asked.

"Not too bad. Looks like you've had a good day. I saw the big load of firewood in the yard."

"That's what I wanted to talk to you about. I don't have a log splitter, but I have an axe. Is there any way you could split that wood for me?"

"Sure. It may take a few days, though. I can even stack it on the front porch for you when I'm done."

"That's good. Thank you very much."

Jeremy finished chopping the wood in about four days.

"The wood's all split and stacked, Mr. Jones. Anything else I can do?"

"Not today. I'll call when I have another job for you. Tell your folks hello for me." Mr. Jones pulled out his wallet. "Here's seventy-five dollars for your work. Thanks again."

"You don't have to do that, but thank you."

"It's the right thing to do. You worked hard."

As time passed, Mr. Jones called Jeremy to cut wood in the fall and mow the grass in the summer. He raked leaves, shoveled snow, and always made sure Mr. Jones had enough firewood inside to keep the woodstove going so he didn't have to go out in the cold. This became a way of life for Jeremy.

In the Boy Scouts, Jeremy was working on earning his merit badges. Unfortunately for him, there wasn't a badge for helping senior citizens. That made no difference to Jeremy. He enjoyed spending time with Mr. Jones, who became like a grandfather to him.

"Jeremy, are you going on the camping trip with the scouts next Friday?" his mom asked.

"No, I don't have time. I've got some brush clearing to do for Mr. Jones."

"But I thought you loved scouting," Mom replied, surprised he would pass up a camping trip.

"Maybe I can make the next one," Jeremy replied as he headed out the door.

This scene played out many times throughout Jeremy's teenage years. He was always working for Mr. Jones and getting paid, but never as much as it was worth; however, Jeremy didn't seem to mind. Mr. Jones also taught Jeremy how to work on cars and build bookshelves and chairs from wood out in his shop.

High school graduation day finally came for Jeremy. Before his family left for the ceremony, Jeremy heard a knock at the front door. He was amazed when he opened it to see Mr. Jones standing there with his walker.

"Hey, Jeremy. May I speak to your parents for a minute?" he asked as he removed his hat and came in.

"Have a seat, and I'll get them for you."

"Good afternoon, Mr. and Mrs. Whitaker. I know you're going to Jeremy's graduation, so I'll only stay a minute. Your son has worked for me since he was old enough to work. I wanted you to know what a good job he has done. He has never asked for money, even though I always gave him a little. He's been like a grandson to me, so I couldn't let him graduate without giving him something."

"You don't have to, Mr. Jones," Dad replied.

"Oh yes, I do. Like I once told Jeremy, it's the right thing to do. He works really hard. Here, Jeremy, this is for you." Mr. Jones handed him an old cigar box.

Jeremy opened the box and stood silently, his mouth wide open.

"Thank you, sir. But I can't take this," he said when he could finally speak.

"Yes, you can. You earned it. Every time you worked for me and I paid you, I put that same amount of money in that old box. There's $2,630.00 in there. I know you missed scouting events and other things, so I promised myself I would take as good care of you as you've taken of me. Thank you. You're a fine young man, and that's the truth. Scout's honor," he said with a grin as he turned to leave.

Sometimes, your efforts are appreciated and rewarded.
Other times, you do stuff just because it's the right thing to do.

DO IT RIGHT THE FIRST TIME

And whatsoever you do, do it heartily,
as to the Lord, and not unto men.
—Colossians 3:23 (KJV)

"Hey, Johnny! I've got an idea. If we rake the leaves over the bank today, we'll have money to go to the game tonight and have all day tomorrow for the fishing tournament."

"Cool, Alan," his brother Johnny replied. "The leaves will be out of Mrs. Thomas's yard, and our weekend plans won't be messed up."

The boys raked as fast as they could. When they finished, they returned Mrs. Thomas's trash bags to her unused.

She was stunned when she opened the door. "What happened to the leaves?"

"We raked them into the gulley, and that way we didn't waste your bags," Alan said.

"Ok. Thanks, boys. The yard does look good. Here's your pay."

"Thanks, Mrs. Thomas," Johnny said, then the boys jumped on their bikes and headed home.

Friday night was cold and windy. When Alan and Johnny returned home from the ball game, Dad met them at the door.

"How was the game?" he asked. The boys responded enthusiastically, telling him about every score. As they went to the garage to get their fishing poles and tackle boxes, Dad stopped them and said, "Mrs. Thomas called while you were gone."

"Did she tell you how good her yard looked when we finished?" Johnny asked, beaming with pride.

"Kind of, but not exactly. She mentioned that you had raked the leaves off into the gulley beside her house, rather than bagging them up as she had asked."

"Yeah, that was my idea," Alan said with a look of satisfaction.

"She also mentioned that the leaves were all over the yard after the wind blew them out of the gulley tonight. I told her you two would be over first thing in the morning to rake them again, and bag them this time," Dad said, obviously displeased with the job they had done.

"We can't do it tomorrow, Dad. We've got a fishing tournament."

"You *had* a fishing tournament. Tomorrow you'll be raking and bagging leaves for free, like Mrs. Thomas already paid you to do. Let this be a lesson for you. There's never time to do it right, but always time to do it over."

Anything worth doing is worth doing right the first time.

NATHAN AND THE LOG SPLITTER

Look not every man on his own things,
but every man also on the things of others.
—Philippians 2:4 (KJV)

"Hi, Nathan. This is Mrs. Miller from next door. Can you cut some firewood for me? I bought some logs, but I need them cut to length and split to go into the woodstove. I'll be glad to pay whatever you charge."

"Glad to. I'll start after school tomorrow. It's supposed to be cold this weekend."

Nathan got his chainsaw and axe from the garage after school the following day, walked next door, and started work. While there, Mr. Jackson called Nathan on his cell phone.

"Good afternoon, Nathan. Are you the one working with the chainsaw at Mrs. Miller's?"

"Yes, sir, that's me. I'm sorry about all the noise. I'll try to hurry."

"Oh, no. That's not what I called about. I have some firewood cut to length but needs to be split. Can you do that?"

"Yes, sir," Nathan replied. "I'll get to it as soon as I finish here."

"How much will you charge to do that?"

"How about I just do it, and you pay me what you think it's worth?"

"Are you sure about that?"

"Yes, sir. We'll settle up when I'm done."

"Mrs. Littrell and Mr. Bowman need their firewood split too. I'll recommend you to them."

"Thank you, sir. I'll call you when I'm done at Mrs. Miller's.

"That'll be fine. Talk to you soon," Mr. Jackson said.

For the next six weeks, Nathan stayed busy cutting and splitting wood for his neighbors. Every time he finished one job, someone else called with another one.

"To celebrate Nathan's sixteenth birthday, his mom decided to throw him a party at the local community center. She invited all the neighbors he had worked for throughout the fall and early winter. To get Nathan into the building, his mom asked him to help decorate for someone's birthday party because the kid's mom needed help.

On the day of the party, Nathan walked into the community center building to find his mom. She had told him that if he helped her decorate, she and his dad would take him out for supper. He thought it strange that all those cars were in the parking lot if the room hadn't even been decorated yet.

"Mom, where are you?" he hollered as he walked from room to room.

"Right here, son," she answered as he came around the corner.

"Surprise! Happy birthday, Nathan," everyone shouted as they emerged from their hiding places.

"What in the world?" he asked in total shock. "How did you all know it was my birthday?"

"Your mom told us. We all went in together and got you something we hope you can use," Mr. Bowman said.

"Someone's knocking. I'll get it." Nathan situated the birthday hat on his head that Mom insisted he wear. He played along with the fun as he opened the door.

"Hey, son. Happy birthday," his dad said. "How about holding the door open for me?" Dad pulled something long and heavy into the room, covered with a tarp and topped with a big bow.

"What's that, Dad? It looks heavy."

"You're right about that. This is from your neighbors. Unwrap it. Everyone's waiting.

Nathan pulled off the tarp. "Are you serious? A ten-horsepower log splitter. Y'all shouldn't have done this. Thank you very much."

"Nathan, you're a hard worker. You've raised blisters on your hands with that axe and wedge. Without us asking, you've carried wood into our houses. We knew you could use this. It's our way of saying thank you and happy birthday," Mrs. Miller explained, then everyone sang the birthday song to him.

"I don't know what to say. You have no idea how many times I've looked at one like this at Mr. Greene's store. I've been saving up to buy it."

"Nathan, I don't have that one anymore. Darndest thing. A man came in the other day and bought it." A sly grin spread across Mr. Greene's face.

"Bet I know who that was." Nathan looked at his dad.

"I'll never tell. But I believe that guy said that he and a bunch of people were buying it for his son." Mr. Greene slapped Nathan on the back. "Happy birthday, Nathan."

Always work hard.
You never know how it will pay off in the end.

WATER-LOGGED

*Servants, be obedient to them that are your masters
according to the flesh, with fear and trembling,
in singleness of your heart, as unto Christ.*
—Ephesians 6:5 (KJV)

"Boss! I need help. I can't hold this coupling and tighten it at the same time. There's too much water," Charlie yelled. Buck jumped into the ditch, splashing Charlie with muddy water as he landed.

"Sorry, Charlie. I didn't mean to drown you. I'll hold it while you tighten the bolts with the pipe wrench." Charlie finally tightened the last bolt and tossed the wrench out of the ditch.

"Whew, that was rough, boss man. That pipe had some serious water pressure. A man needs three hands to get one of those compression couplings on by himself." Charlie leaned against the side of the ditch to catch his breath.

"You did good, Charlie. You could probably use a little more weight on your backside before you try doing a man's job."

"A man's job! Are you kidding me? That's a two-man job if there's ever been one."

Buck laughed as he bent over and cupped his hands together for Charlie to climb up out of the ditch.

"Now, how are you getting out, boss man?"

"I'm taking the elevator. I'm too old to be climbing out of ditches. That's for you young guys that don't know any better."

"What elevator?

Buck grinned. "Just tell Jerry to bring the elevator over here, and I'll show you."

"Whatever you say, boss."

A couple of minutes later, Jerry backed the backhoe near the ditch and dropped the rear bucket into it beside Buck.

"First floor, please, sir." Buck stepped into the bucket. "See, I told you there was an elevator," he said as he stepped out onto the ground beside Charlie.

"As usual, you were right, boss man. All joking aside, why on earth did you jump down there in your good clothes?"

"It's like this, son," Buck said while drying off with a towel. "When Mr. Bowman hired me, I was about your age. I promised him I'd always do my best, so he'd never regret giving me a chance. I give him an honest day's work, and then some, for an honest day's pay. He's promoted and given me raises over the years, so I guess he's still satisfied with my work."

"Maybe so, but I doubt he expects you to jump into a ditch full of muddy water with your good clothes on. You've been around here for years. He's not about to let you go."

"I know he doesn't expect stuff like that, but anything less wouldn't be my best, and I don't ever want to break my promise." Buck climbed in the truck. "Plus, with a clear conscience, I sleep like a baby at night."

You never get too old to do your best.

THE BROKEN GLASS

Be sure your sin will find you out.
—Numbers 32:23 (KJV)

Eli Johnson's store had been closed for years. His grandson now owned the old building but lived out of state. Vagrants slept in it during bad weather, but it served no purpose to anyone else.

Mason and Lewis rode past it daily on their bikes going to school. Boys will be boys, and boys will throw rocks. The windows in that old place seemed irresistible. Even though they knew better, they began throwing rocks. When the first window shattered, that was all she wrote. They competed to see who could throw the farthest and hit one. Then it was how many they could throw without missing. By the time their game ended, every window was broken.

The boys thought no more about it until they were called to the principal's office the following day. "Boys," Principal Johnson said, "all the windows in my uncle's old store were broken yesterday. I know you ride home that way. Did you see someone throwing rocks?"

"No. That's terrible!" Mason said.

Lewis shook his head. "We didn't see anything."

When they got home, their dad also told them about the windows. "If you see anyone around there, let me know."

"Ok, Dad, we will," Lewis said.

"Thanks, boys. I knew I could count on you."

Mason nodded. "Sure thing, Dad."

"Principal Johnson's cousin had an offer on the property, but now he'll have to replace all the windows before the sale goes through."

Although a guilty conscience was nagging at both boys, they kept their secret. No one asked if they'd done it, only if they'd seen anything.

The guilt, however, grew worse. Dad saw it on their faces. Rather than call their hand about it, he let them stew a while and get a little more miserable.

A couple of weeks passed, and the boys couldn't stand it any longer. They decided to donate some of their lawn-mowing money to help pay for the windows. As their dad watched the news that evening, they gave him money and told him they wanted to help with the windows.

"That's good of you two. I'm sure ol' man Johnson's son will appreciate it. Although I'm proud of you, you probably should've thought it through a little more before you broke all those windows."

"How did you know, Dad? Mason asked.

"We didn't say anything to anyone!" Lewis added.

"First off, I've seen that guilty look before, and second, you shouldn't have dropped your ball cap behind the store, Lewis. I found it when I stopped to investigate the damage to the building that evening. We'll worry about punishment after you pay for the windows. Maybe next time you'll remember to respect other people's property.

Just because you can, doesn't mean you should.

FRIENDSHIP

Eight stories that show you can't put a price on friendship.

Walter Winchell, a former American syndicated newspaper gossip columnist and radio news commentator, gave a wonderful definition for a friend. "A real friend is one who walks in when the rest of the world walks out." Dictionary.com defines friend as "a person attached to another by feelings of affection or personal regard." Another definition says, "one who gives assistance." A friend supports you in whatever way is needed.

No one likes to be around unpleasant or dishonest people. The Bible says in James 1:8, "A double-minded man is unstable in all his ways" (KJV). Down home, that kind of person is called two-faced. They can't be trusted with secrets or even accuracy in general conversation. Gossiping and lying are dangerous traits that cannot be tolerated in a meaningful friendship.

True friends keep conversations confidential and carry them to their graves. As defined by Walter Winchell, a friend stands by their friends regardless of the circumstances. They're there in good times and bad, either physically or in conversation. Giving and accepting advice is also part of a trusted friendship. In my opinion, a friend is someone who can be trusted to tell you when you're wrong without being judgmental. They can also be counted on to help correct whatever the situation is. Friends don't desert you, no matter what happens or what the opinions of others may be. Time and distance mean little to a faithful friend. If needed, they'll move heaven and earth to meet a friend's needs. Down home, those people are called true-blue friends.

Sometimes all that's needed is a sympathetic ear. My best friend from childhood would be on my doorstep with only a phone call if he thought I needed something. Once we became teenagers, people usually saw us together on weekends and school vacations. We sat up nearly all night with our brothers playing poker. He once stayed with me till 3:00 a.m. after a girlfriend broke up with me. I didn't need advice, and he said very little. Companionship was all I needed that night. I was the same way with him. When your heart is broken, a true friend hurts with you.

After graduating from high school, we took a trip together. We spent many hours on a Greyhound, seeing the country, cutting up, and having many conversations we would never share with anyone else. We worked together, camped, hunted, and fished together, and spent many weekends at each other's homes for years. He was practically another brother, except in many ways closer. We were at each other's wedding and were always each other's first call when something good or bad happened in our lives. We were present for each other's hospital stays and the birth of our sons. Even now, when tragedy invades our lives, we can count on each other to show up and be there like we always have.

Loyal friends are always the first to run to your defense and the last to criticize. A loyal friend doesn't always have to agree with you but is always understanding when you don't see eye-to-eye. You can agree to disagree and still keep your relationship. Faithful friends never abandon you because of disagreements. They believe in and support you, even when no one else does.

Another wonderful thing about true friendship is that you never have to try to impress the other person. You can be yourself and completely at ease. A friend encourages and never disparages you when you try new things. They lay out the facts and encourage you to examine all the evidence before making decisions.

Proverbs 18:24 says, "A man that hath friends must shew himself friendly" (KJV). Simply put, to have friends, be one. Defining a true friend is hard, but over time, they become woven into the fabric of our lives. We all know the traits we look for and admire in our friends. Can our friends find those same qualities in us?

In the following stories, you'll see several of these characteristics displayed and their effect on both parties involved. The stories aren't a how-to guide for making friends. They do, however, show the effort involved in friendship. Like any relationship, it takes a lot of work and often even more understanding and forgiveness. As you read, ask yourself, "What kind of friend am I?"

BROKEN CRAYONS

Inasmuch as ye have done it unto one of the least of
these my brethren, ye have done it unto me.
—Matthew 35:40 (KJV)

Five-year-old Stevie jumped out of bed, excited about starting school and riding the big yellow bus. Now he would have plenty of boys to play with. Before he knew it, he was jostling in his seat as the bus rumbled to the corner and stopped at Fifth and Elm Street. Peering out the window, he watched as the bus driver helped a kid in a wheelchair board the bus. The only place to lock down the boy's chair happened to be right beside Stevie. He turned and smiled, "Hi, I'm Stevie."

The little boy responded with a surprised look and a wide, toothless grin.

"My name's Ralph. I'm in second grade."

As the bus's brakes screeched and it pulled to a stop in front of the school, Stevie tapped Ralph on the shoulder. "How about I carry your backpack? It looks heavy."

Eager for his first day of school, Stevie struggled up the steps as his new friend took the ramp. That's when it happened—the top step seemed to jump up and trip him. Sprawled on the sidewalk, an embarrassed Stevie scrambled to gather everything that had spilled from Ralph's backpack.

"At least your box of crayons didn't fly open," Stevie said as he picked up the box and opened it. He gasped when he looked inside. "I'm sorry. I broke all your crayons, but I have a box at home I can bring you."

"Don't worry, I have more. No big deal," Ralph assured him as they went inside. After rolling down the hall, he spun around, waved, and shouted, "I'll see you on the bus."

The following day, when Ralph got on the bus, Stevie said, "Close your eyes. I have a surprise for you."

When Ralph looked up, his eyes got as big as saucers, and his whole face erupted into a big, toothless smile. "Wow, thanks. You didn't need to give me your crayons." He opened the box and began breaking each one.

As he looked on in horror, Stevie shouted, "Ralph, what are you doing?"

"Oh, I'm sorry," he said with a chuckle. "It's not that I'm ungrateful, but I guess I should explain myself."

"Last year in first grade, a few older boys liked to pick on me. They dumped my backpack in the hall, broke my crayons, and then walked away laughing because there was nothing I could do about it. Some other kids picked everything up and then walked me to class."

"As I rolled into homeroom, my teacher handed me a picture and said, 'Here, Ralph. Color this for me. Use your imagination and any colors you want.' I was sad because my crayons were all broken, but I had no choice but to use them. The other kids laughed when they saw them."

My teacher felt sorry for me and brought me a new box of crayons from her desk. I looked at my picture and the broken crayon in my hand. I figured out that with my bent hand, I couldn't control a long crayon. But the broken crayon fit nicely into my hand, giving me complete control, so I broke the new crayons. As I did, she got angry and was about to send me to the office, but looking at my picture, she said, "You do incredible coloring for a first grader."

"I broke all my crayons. Not only could I color better, but I liked the smaller crayons. I broke my pencils, too, with the eraser end short like my crayons, so I could hold them. My writing improved, and my teacher said I had the best printing in the whole first grade." He straightened in his wheelchair, threw back his shoulders, and grinned. "I even won the penmanship award."

Stevie's eyes bulged. "Wow! That all happened because some bullies broke your crayons? That's unbelievable!"

"I draw all kinds of stuff. If you ever want me to draw something for you, just let me know." Proud that his new friend had bragged about him, Ralph reached into his backpack and pulled out a drawing of a horse. "Here you go. You can have this."

"Thanks," Stevie said. "Those bullies helped you more than they hurt you. This is a great picture. You're really good."

Just because something is broken,
doesn't mean it's useless.

PAYBACK OR PEACE OF MIND?

Recompense to no man evil for evil.
Provide things honest in the sight of all men.
—Romans 12:17 (KJV)

Harold got a lump in his throat when he punched the clock for the last time. His coworkers lined up to say their goodbyes. It wasn't a retirement party. After thirty-four years with the company, he had been replaced by someone younger, with no experience. The replacement's degree in literary studies in no way qualified him to be a machine shop supervisor. But it was cheaper for the company to hire a greenhorn fresh out of college than to pay Harold a well-deserved higher salary for his experience. The new guy would also grow old one day and be replaced with a younger, inexperienced person.

Harold had started the job when he was twenty-four years old. He swept floors and was a maintenance assistant for three years while studying machine shop at the local community college in the evenings. When he earned his degree, the company hired him as a machinist. After fifteen years in that position, he was promoted to line supervisor. Seven years later, Harold became the production manager of the whole shop.

There wasn't a more beloved boss than Harold. He treated his workers like family—attending their weddings, funerals, and birthday parties. He gave gifts for every worker's personal occasions. His employees were all treated with respect and compassion. Harold even filled in when they had to leave for family emergencies or other appointments, which meant he often stayed late to catch up on his own work.

His department had the fewest turnovers in the plant. But none of that mattered today. A gold watch, a severance package, and a boot out the door were all he received. All the other employees realized a similar fate awaited them when they gained a few years of seniority. The brass wouldn't admit it, but the old timers saw the retirement plan for what it was—a way to get rid of an older, higher-paid worker and save money.

Sometime later, a coworker received his dismissal and came to Harold for advice. "If I had my way, I'd get even," the coworker growled.

Harold scratched his head. "Let it go. It's hard, but vengeance isn't your job. That belongs to God, and He always takes care of His children. You'll see. Move on and seek out the joy in your life."

Months later, Harold heard news that didn't surprise him. Due to the inadequate quality of the workmanship on their products, the plant lost two major accounts. They were forced to lay off the younger members of management on a permanent basis. Harold was right all along. A literary master's degree doesn't qualify anyone to supervise a machine shop. "There's no substitute for experience," Harold whispered as he closed the newspaper. God does repay.

Never allow circumstances to make you bitter.
Let them make you better.

IT DOESN'T MATTER WHO THROWS YOU THE ROPE

A man that hath friends must shew himself friendly: and there is a friend that sticketh closer than a brother.
—Proverbs 18:24 (KJV)

Graduation had finally arrived. Tony and Devon graduated with honors. Tony was a middle-class white kid; Devon came from the projects. Both played tailback, each finishing with over 1,000 yards their senior year.

Tony had a partial academic scholarship but chose a stint in the Navy instead. Devon beat the odds, earning a full ride to a Division 1 school on a football scholarship. They took separate paths but always cherished their memories and remained each other's strongest supporters.

Four years later, Tony left the Navy and enlisted in the reserves. He entered a top school, continuing his Navy specialty in electromagnetics. Devon didn't make the National Football League, but he was drafted by the Canadian League. The two friends stayed close, pushing each other toward greatness.

Five years after graduation, Tony's mom called Devon. Tony had been injured in the reserves and was hooked on pain meds. If anyone could reach him, it would be Devon. After wiping away tears for his friend, Devon promised to come to see Tony.

Devon leaned back in the seat before takeoff, recalling where he'd been months earlier. He'd blown out his knee in training camp. As always, he called Tony with the news. On surgery day, his doorbell rang. He opened the door to see his old friend Tony standing there with a suitcase and a big smile.

"Training camp starts immediately following your therapy. You'll be eating right, and I'm going to whip you back into shape. You're too young and too good to think of quitting. Are you going to invite me in, or do I have to get a hotel?" Tony asked.

Devon had a loyal friend in Tony. Now, it was his turn. The stakes were much higher because Tony had much more to lose. *We're about to face our toughest challenge yet.* Devon knew Tony's mom was right. If anyone could reach Tony, he could. After all, that's what friends were for. Tony had saved his career. Now, he'd try to save Tony's life.

Tony flung open the door. "What do you want?" he yelled, rubbing sleep from his eyes.

"It's my turn now, T-Man," Devon said, smiling. "Rehab starts now. I'm gonna be your worst nightmare and whip you into shape. You're too young and too good to even think about quitting life." Tony bear-hugged Devon, sobbing uncontrollably.

"I don't know what to do, man," Tony said.

"That's what I'm here for. We'll get through this together, just like we have since kindergarten."

A few months later, Devon wiped tears while accepting a plaque that read Canadian Football League Comeback Player of the Year. The league flew Tony in to present the award.

Standing shoulder to shoulder on stage during a rousing ovation, they couldn't believe how their lives had unfolded. Devon, the Black kid from the projects of East Tutleyville, had run his way into the hearts of football fans all over Canada. In Devon's mind, though, Tony had overcome much more adversity than he had.

Both young men had stood by their friend when needed. Tony had gone from middle-class white suburbia to the gutter and back with Devon's help, and Devon now stood on a stage in Montreal, having overcome a career-ending knee injury. But he believed the biggest winner was standing beside him.

Devon stepped to the podium and began his speech. "I'm not much on speeches, but I want you all to know something about me. Without Tony, I wouldn't be here today. When I blew out my knee, the morning of the surgery, he was standing at my door telling me how brutal he was going to be in my rehab. As you know, he made good on his threats. When you're drowning and need rescuing, it doesn't matter who throws you the rope, so I want to dedicate this award to him. I'm thankful he stood by me then and is standing by me now. God bless y'all and thank you very much for the award."

A true friend runs in when everyone else is running out.

FRECKLES

Thou shalt not steal.
—Exodus 20:15 (KJV)

No one knew where the old dog came from or even what kind of dog he was. The construction crew thought he might be part Dalmatian with all his spots, but he was too small for that. He had showed up on the job site one day around lunchtime. He had no collar, so the crew adopted him and named him Freckles.

Every morning he waited by the gate for the crew to arrive. Often, they tossed him the last bite of their biscuit and rubbed his head. They talked about someone taking him home but decided to fix him a place of his own, out of the weather. They chipped in their change each week to buy Freckles food. One man even bought him a fluorescent orange collar that said, "Freckles." The men joked if they had to wear safety orange, Freckles should too.

The job foreman took a liking to Freckles and brought him bacon treats daily. The dog stayed on the boss's heels everywhere he went.

"Here, Freckles. Come and get your bacon," John said as he set his lunchbox down in the office and got his hard hat. "If they made these for dogs, you'd have to wear one too." John headed out the door, his trusty companion right on his heels as usual.

At quitting time that evening, everyone passed by the office to pet Freckles. Once they left, Freckles had the place to himself. He wandered about the construction yard looking for scraps and acting like he owned the place. After a few more sips from his water bowl and scarfing down the last of his supper, he stretched out on the hay in the shed John had put beside his office, then drifted off to sleep.

Waking suddenly from sleep at two in the morning, Freckles perked his ears up. Two men were talking. Getting up from his bed and stretching, he crept toward the voices, keeping close to the building. The supply trailer door stood open, so he investigated. Two men in hoodies were going through the trailer, taking stuff. With a low growl, Freckles stood firmly in the doorway, his hackles raised.

"Go away, you mangy old mutt. We're busy here," one of the thieves said.

The old dog began barking, only stopping to throw in a growl.

"We've got to go," one thief told the other as he started toward the door.

Freckles lunged at the man, forcing him to back up.

"We're trapped," he told his partner. "Do you have any ideas?"

"Yes, I do," the other man replied. "Here's our ticket out: a whole box of bacon treats."

Proud of his discovery, the thief started throwing them out the door one by one. He threw some right under the dog's nose, but Freckles didn't move an inch. He growled more viciously and barked even louder.

"Alright, you boys come out of there, and don't try anything stupid. If we don't get you, I think this dog will," a police officer said, pointing his gun at the thieves.

"Good boy," another officer told Freckles. His partner picked up a bacon strip from the ground and held it out to the dog. He took it gently, chewed it, and began picking up the rest of them while the officers handcuffed the suspects.

The following morning, the officers stopped by the job site when their shift ended.

"Hey, John. We caught two guys in your trailer last night and arrested them. That's a good watchdog you have."

"I don't have a watchdog. All we have is Freckles. Hang on. Let me call him. Freckles, come here, boy."

While the officer told John the story, old Freckles trotted slowly around the building.

"That's him," Officer Rickman explained as Freckles went to him to be petted.

"Are you serious? Freckles caught two guys in the supply trailer?"

"Oh yeah," Officer Berman chimed in. "We stopped at the light and heard a dog barking, so we climbed the back fence and eased in. This dog had the suspects trapped in the trailer. They tried to get him to back away by throwing bacon strips to him, but he never moved. There was bacon everywhere, but I swear that dog didn't touch any of it until those guys were in cuffs."

"That's a good dog you've got there," Officer Rickman said as he scratched Freckles behind his ears. "He sure saved you a bunch of money."

"We didn't think he'd bite a biscuit," John said with pride, reaching down to pet him.

"Those two thieves would probably disagree," Officer Berman said.

All three men laughed.

Be kind to animals.
They may take care of you when you least expect it.

THE MOWER AND THE BLACKSNAKE

But whoso hath this world's good, and seeth his brother have need, and shutteth up his bowels of compassion from him, how dwelleth the love of God in him.
—1 John 3:17 (KJV)

"Daddy, that snake just bit me," Sandy cried as she ran toward the house.

"Where was it? Her dad jumped to his feet.

"By the apple tree. I didn't do anything to it. Tommy and me were just playing on the swing."

"I see it. It's a blacksnake, but we'll take you to the doctor to ensure the bite doesn't get infected."

After they returned home, Sandy's dad, Landon, went to Dajon's small engine shop.

"Hi, Landon. Interested in buying a mower? I've got some good used ones in stock that I've rebuilt."

"I brought mine to see if you could fix it. Sandy got bitten by a blacksnake this morning, and I've got to cut the long grass at the back of my property."

Dajon pulled the crank on Landon's mower a couple of times and checked the spark plug.

"When was the last time you put in a new spark plug? This one's burnt up, but you've got bigger problems. Sounds like the crankshaft's broken." Dajon rubbed his chin. "Can't say for sure 'til I tear it apart."

"I was afraid you'd say something like that."

"I can let you know something by tomorrow evening. Stop by on your way home from work." Dajon pulled a new push mower from the back row of his shop. "Meanwhile, why don't you take this one home and get that grass cut before Tommy finds a snake too?"

"I can't do that, Dajon. It's brand new, and I couldn't afford to buy it if I tore it up. Thanks anyway."

"I insist. I assembled it this morning but haven't had time to try it out. You'd be doing me a favor. Let me know if it gives you any problems."

"Thanks, Dajon, if you're sure about this."

"I'm sure. I'll even help you load it."

When they were finished loading the mower, Landon turned to shake Dajon's hand. "Thanks again. I'll take good care of it."

"Just let me know how it runs. I hope Sandy will be alright."

"I'm sure she will be. I will be, too, when I get that grass cut. That ought to calm June down a bit. You know how it is, if Momma ain't happy, ain't nobody happy," Landon called as he backed out onto the road.

The next day, Landon stopped by Dajon's shop on his way home.

"That mower worked great. I don't know when my grass has ever looked that good. What's the good word on my old junker?"

"It didn't survive. Between the crankshaft and the coil, it was shot. A new crankshaft would cost more than a new mower. I'd say you've got your money's worth out of it. That thing's been around a day or two."

"I've had that since June and I bought the house. It's older than either of the kids." Landon laughed. "Guess that's almost fifteen years. I'll return your mower tomorrow."

"I'll call you when I need it. It wouldn't be doing anything except sitting around here if you brought it back. Somebody might as well use it," Dajon said.

"Are you sure?"

Dajon smiled. "I wish you'd quit asking me that. After all the times June babysat Brian when he was a colicky baby, loaning you a mower is the least I can do. Nikki and I appreciated June's help so much."

Later that night at supper, Nikki said, "June called and told me about Sandy getting snakebit and that you loaned Landon a mower. I know you won't ever ask for it back. You're too bighearted for your own good sometimes." She leaned over and patted his hand. "But that's one of the things I love about you. If you can do something to help someone, you do. That makes me proud of you."

"Shush that talk, woman. You're gonna make me blush." Dajon grinned. "It's just a mower. I can always get another one."

Landon walked toward the shed to put the gas can away. "That ol' blacksnake sure picked the wrong young'un to bite this time. He won't ever have tall grass to roam around in now."

A friend in need is a friend indeed.

FREE CHOCOLATE

Children obey your parents in all things:
for this is well pleasing unto the Lord.
—Colossians 3:20 (KJV)

"Hey, Martin. Are you selling candy for the school fundraiser?"

"Sure am, Rodney. The caramel is my favorite." Martin held up his box of candy bars.

"Mine too. Fifth grade isn't selling candy this year."

"That's too bad. If you wanna buy any, I'll sell you one."

"I don't have any money until I get my allowance on Friday. Can I get one now and pay you then?"

"Sure thing. Today's Monday. I guess I can wait until Friday." Martin gladly handed over a candy bar. "See you tomorrow."

"Thanks, Martin," Rodney waved goodbye, walking toward the bus and wiping caramel from his chin.

"Hi, Mom." Martin raced to his mom in the kitchen. "We got our candy bars today at school. I'm going to sell more than anyone else and win the grand prize—a big red remote-controlled car."

"That's wonderful, son. Put the money in your room, and don't carry it to school. And don't give candy bars to your friends, or you'll have to pay for them," Mom called out as Martin ran upstairs.

"Okay," he replied, running back downstairs and outside to sell candy to his neighbors. After going through the cul-de-sac, he returned home with a pocket full of crumpled-up one-dollar bills.

"I'm back, Mom," he shouted as he ran up to his room.

"Supper's almost ready. Wash up and come to the table after you put your money away."

The next morning, Rodney was waiting for Martin when he got off the school bus. "Morning, Martin. Do you still have any candy bars left?" Rodney gave him a fist bump.

"A few. I sold most of them after school yesterday."

"You must be a good salesman. Can I get another one and pay you more on Friday?"

"Sure, but I'm out of caramels."

"Chocolate Crunch is fine with me."

"Here you go. I'll see you after school."

That scene replayed all week. Rodney had paid no money, but Martin kept giving him candy bars. Four in all. On Friday morning, Rodney saw Martin approaching him and went the other way. Confused, Martin wondered if Rodney was mad at him. He saw Rodney again after school, going to the bus.

"Hey, Rodney. I need the money for the candy bars. It's due Monday."

"Sorry, Martin. My dad only gets paid every other week. I won't get my allowance until next Friday. I can pay you then."

How could Rodney tell him a lie and not pay him? Martin knew he'd be in trouble when he got home, and his parents counted his money.

"Hey, son. How was school?" Mom asked from the kitchen.

"Ok, I guess," Martin said, heading to his room.

"Bring your candy money down when you come for supper, and we'll count it."

"Alright, Mom." Martin took his piggy bank from the bookshelf. Only one dollar and twenty-five cents. He still needed two dollars and seventy-five cents to make up for the money Rodney owed him. He let out a long sigh, then took all the money downstairs.

After supper, Mom counted it. "Martin, why are you two dollars and seventy-five cents short? Did you give candy bars away after I told you not to? That wasn't your money to spend, son. You'll have to pay the difference."

"Rodney said he was going to pay me today when he got his allowance. He figured out later that he wouldn't get it until next Friday when his dad gets paid."

"Young man, you'll help your dad clean the garage tomorrow to earn money for the candy. And next Saturday, you'll help me in the garden. In the meantime, you'll be grounded. Do I make myself clear?" Mom's face turned redder by the minute.

"But, Mom, you said you might let me go fishing with Skip and his dad."

"No arguing, son. When you don't do what you're told, you don't get to do things you want to do."

Martin took his shower and went to bed early, still mad because he wasn't going fishing. Giving those candy bars to Rodney got him in a lot of trouble. Working two Saturdays instead of playing made Martin miserable. What made it worse was that Rodney never paid him. Not only was he grounded, but he had disobeyed and disappointed his parents, which made him feel terrible. Martin liked working with his parents, but all that work and trouble was a high price to pay for free chocolate.

Sometimes people are only your friends
for what they can get from you.

YOU NEVER KNOW

As we have, therefore, opportunity,
let us do good unto all men.
—Galatians 6:10(KJV)

"Howdy, neighbor. I'm Stan. I live over on the main road and saw y'all moving in. Welcome to the neighborhood."

"I'm Buddy. That's the coolest bike I've ever seen. Sparkly red and a 3-speed shifter. I've never seen one like it before."

"Thanks, Buddy. Do you want to ride it down your driveway?"

"Wow. Can I really?"

"Sure. I'll wait right here."

So was born an enduring friendship. Stan and Buddy spent long summer days riding their bikes together, playing cowboys and Indians, and pretending those bikes were horses. Buddy's bike was an old, beat-up landfill special. He got it on a trip to the county dump with his uncle, who helped him fix it up.

Long summer days turned into a couple of years. Buddy and his family moved to a new school district, and the boys lost touch.

Years later, a man walked into Buddy's auto repair shop.

"Good morning, sir. What can I do for you?" Buddy reached out to shake hands.

"Need my old truck checked out. It's getting hard to start and running a bit sluggish, like me. We both have a lot of miles on us."

The stranger shook Buddy's hand. "I'm Stan."

"You look awfully familiar, Stan. Are you from around here?"

"I grew up on Aiken Road. Left for college years ago and just moved back."

"What a coincidence. I grew up there too. Wait a minute, I know you. You had the red 3-speed Schwinn Stingray with the chrome sissy bar and the red banana seat. You took up for me when I got picked on riding the school bus." He shook his head. "It really is a small world."

"Are you Buddy?"

"I am. We moved away after second grade, and I always wondered what happened to you." Another man walked up and stood beside Buddy. "Do you remember my big brother Kevin?"

Stan nodded. "Good to see you, Kevin."

"So, you're a mechanic now, Buddy?" Stan asked.

"Yes, sir. I started this shop not long after I finished diesel school. Kevin runs it. I just happened to be off the road today, giving my Peterbilt a wash job and tune-up."

"That's your metallic red truck out there? I should've guessed. You sure liked my bike when we were kids."

"Couldn't resist the red and the chrome stacks either." Buddy grinned.

"What brings you back to town, Stan?"

"I retired. Thought I'd move back, maybe find something different, and start a second career."

"Ever considered truck driving? I'd be glad to show you the ropes and help you get your Class A Commercial Driver's License. I could use a co-driver."

"Are you serious?" Stan asked. "I've always wanted to travel, and that way, I could do it and get paid too. Sounds like a winner."

"Get a driver's handbook and your Class A learner's permit. I'm leaving on Monday for Seattle if that works for you."

"Sure does."

"I'll check your truck, and you can pick it up tomorrow. Next week, we'll start working on making you a professional tourist like me," Buddy said.

They left the following Monday, and Stan began his new life. Six weeks later, he walked out of the driver's license office with a big grin and asked Buddy, "Who says you can't teach an old dog new tricks?"

Both men were still laughing as they drove down the road. Buddy looked at Stan and said, "Who would've ever thought we'd get back together after all this time? The only difference is now we're riding my truck instead of your bike. You just never know."

Be kind to other people.
You may gain a lifelong friend.

BUSTED

For there is nothing hid, which shall not be
manifested; neither was anything kept secret, but
that it should come abroad.
—Mark 4:22 (KJV)

Alvin's buddies stood at the corner of the building. Larry's brother had given him a joint, and he was sharing it with the guys. They'd all been friends since elementary school—played Little League together, joined the Boy Scouts, and spent most of their summer days swimming in the big hole in Rock Bottom Creek. Thick as thieves, as the old saying goes. Where you saw one, the rest weren't far behind.

Alvin didn't want to get laughed at, but he didn't want to try marijuana either. It would soon be his turn, and so far, everyone had done it. He was one of the leaders of the group because he was a senior. Still, he had college to worry about, and more importantly, what if his mom found out? He could imagine her disappointment, her crying, blaming herself, and wondering where she had gone wrong.

Alvin's parents divorced when he was six years old. He rarely saw his dad. Mom had struggled to raise three kids alone and always worked at least two jobs. Alvin, at nearly seventeen, was the man of the house. Preston was thirteen, Carla eleven. Alvin wondered what his siblings would say if they found out he had smoked a joint. How could he face them again?

As Larry passed the joint to Alvin, it was decision time. "You know what, Larry? I'm not gonna try that, and y'all shouldn't either," he said.

"Look who's being goody-two-shoes all of a sudden." Larry laughed as the others stared at the ground. One by one, they walked away.

"Since when did you become a wimp?" Larry asked Alvin.

"Nothing wimpy about it. I started thinking about how I would face Mom, Preston, and Carla. If I got caught, I don't think I could look any of them in the eye again. Sorry, buddy, but there are a lot more important things in life than a little bit of weed," Alvin replied sharply, a little angry about being called a wimp.

"You've got exams coming up too," Alvin added. "You need to keep your head clear. Besides, a drug charge could ruin your admission to the Air Force Academy. Even if they accepted you, you'd likely lose your dream of being a fighter pilot. Marijuana isn't worth all of that," Alvin said as he slung his backpack on. "Think about it, man. You've got a lot to lose. We'd better get to class before we're late."

"Good point, Alvin. Are you sure you aren't going to be a lawyer?" Larry chuckled as they went their separate ways. When he got his backpack and rounded the corner, Larry looked up right into the face of Principal Stroupe.

"Larry," he said sternly. "Tell me I'm not smelling weed on you. And you better not lie to me, boy."

"Well, sir, you caught me. I wouldn't think of lying to you, sir," Larry replied.

"This is what's going to happen now, young man. Because you're being honest with me, and I know you've applied to the Air Force Academy, I'll let you off with a warning. But if I ever catch you so much as late to class, I'll nail your hide to the wall! Do I make myself clear?"

"Oh, yes sir, sir. You'll never catch me smelling like weed again, I promise."

"Alright, Larry. This'll be our secret. But remember what I said. One more problem and you'll be cleaning toilets with the custodians until you graduate, understood?"

"Yes, sir, Mr. Stroupe. You can count on me."

"You better be right, Larry. One drug charge, and you can kiss a cockpit goodbye for at least one more year."

"Yes, sir. I know. Alvin told me that on his way to class."

"Alvin, huh? Listen to him. He's a good friend. A true friend is strong enough to tell you when you're wrong."

"Yes, sir! He's definitely a true friend," Larry hollered back as he ran off to class.

Just because everyone else does it doesn't mean you should.

WHERE THERE IS LIFE, THERE'S HOPE

Five stories proving that if you're living, you're never without hope.

Hippocrates, the Greek philosopher, once said, "Desperate times call for desperate measures." That's another one of our sayings down-home, although I never knew who said it when I was young. It's one of those we don't like to become too well acquainted with. None of us enjoy those times, but it's those tough situations that build our character. As far as I'm concerned, I could make do with a little less character and a lot more leisure.

From the pioneer days in the mountains of western North Carolina, life around here has been marked by poverty. Often, it was related to poor soil or, even more so, the terrain, which made growing crops difficult at best. The lifestyle of early settlers in western North Carolina came to be called *hardscrabble*. The word is a combination of two words—difficult or arduous and scrabble, which came to mean scratching or clawing out a life under rough circumstances.

The unique aspect of life in the Southern Appalachian Mountains is that most people had the same life. No one knew they were poor because they lived like everybody else. It was just life, and that's how it was. Mountain people often didn't travel far outside their community in their lifetime, if at all.

In the late 1980s or early 1990s, I met an old gentleman at the only factory in a small town called Plumtree, NC. It was named by the earliest settlers who found hundreds of wild plum trees along the North Toe River area of Avery County. I was a truck driver making a delivery there when the older man struck up a conversation. He asked what Asheville, NC, was like. He told me he hadn't been to Asheville, about sixty-five miles away, in around forty years. When I asked why, he said he never had a good reason to go. He said it had been a long time since he'd been to Spruce Pine, about fifteen miles away. I was in my early twenties with a bad case of wanderlust. I couldn't believe a man his age hadn't been out of Plumtree in decades, but it was common for someone not to travel without a good reason. The hardscrabble life was filled with hard labor and meager supplies in this a poverty-stricken region. The term is still used for people who seem to have their backs against the wall constantly. Those who go from one desperate situation to another and claw their way out only to wind up in a worse circumstance. Not everyone who endures difficult times in their hardscrabble life is there because of poor decisions, although some are. Others seem to have been dealt a bad hand or continuously have a run of bad luck. No matter the reason or circumstance, we must push through those tough situations. The stories in this section cover many scenarios, time periods, and people of various ages. The one characteristic these people share is a never-say-die attitude.

The stories cover many of the same circumstances people face today. Everything from factory closings, health issues, and problems in the home. There are also struggling teens, a scared little girl making her way home from school in a storm, and a man who has lost his home and is living in his car with his family. Another is a young mom with a low income, several kids, and an injured, unemployed husband. Like most of us, some folks in the stories deal with mean people.

All these folks experienced what has come to be known as Murphy's Law: "Anything that can go wrong will." These stories have a few things in common. First, there's an element of truth in each of them. Another commonality is that just when things became as bad as the person thought possible, the situation got worse. Each story also holds the slightest thread of hope when circumstances seem the worst. Unlike life, these stories all have a happy ending. The struggles the people face may continue, but each person reaches a level of peace and contentment because of hope.

Your life story is no different. Despite any difficulties you might face or how hardscrabble your life may become, you too still have that tiny shred of hope. One phrase in the Bible appears four hundred and fifty-two times and is still as true as when it was written: "it came to pass." No matter what storms you may face in life, "it came to pass." They're only temporary, not permanent. These stories illustrate that even when situations look impossible and hopeless, where there is life, there is hope.

LORD, HAVE MERCY

Let us therefore come boldly unto the throne of grace, that we may obtain mercy, and find grace to help in time of need.
—Hebrews 4:16 (KJV)

Thump, thump, thump! Her car was driving like a tank as she pulled to the shoulder of the road. Stepping into the cold rain, Leann stared helplessly at the rear tire. The belts that had been showing for weeks had finally given way. Couldn't have happened at a worse time. She had worked late and left the kids with the babysitter a little longer. Christmas was coming, and her three kids hoped Santa wouldn't forget them.

Little did they know Santa had a blowout on the way to pick them up. Three little ones—ages four, two, and one—wouldn't remember that upcoming Christmas with small gifts, if any, but she would. If she had to buy a new tire, the extra money she'd made from working overtime would be gone with the wind. She could do nothing but cry and pray as she stood on the roadside in the cold rain and darkness.

"Lord, why this and why now? I'm trying to raise my kids right, keep them fed and in church. I'm doing everything I can do."

Since their father died in combat a year before, Leann had struggled to be both mom and dad. Now, cold, soaked, and alone, she was exhausted, consumed with despair, and on the verge of giving up when a pair of headlights pierced the darkness.

Brian Black pulled his rollback to a stop in front of her car. "Ms. Leann," he said, "I'm no knight in shining armor, but I am a flunky with a rollback. How about you get up in my truck and stay warm while I load your car? Then I'll take you home."

"Thank you, Brian! I need to call the babysitter and let her know how late I'll be." "No need for that," Brian replied. "We'll swing by and get the kids on the way. They'd probably like to ride in my truck anyway. I'll even put their car seats in the back seat."

One long hour later, and finally in dry clothes, Leann got the kids in bed and collapsed in her chair. Suddenly, the door flung open!

"Whew, that rain's not letting up, but I got your tire changed."

"Oh gosh, you scared me. I forgot you were out there. How much do I owe you, Brian?"

"Sorry, I didn't mean to scare you. If you give me a hot cup of coffee, we'll call it even, Ms. Leann."

Moments later, as she watched the taillights fade in the distance, she thought about her night. She'd seen Brian a few times at church but hadn't spoken much more than hello. Yet this caring stranger had rescued her in the rain. All it cost her was a cup of coffee.

Two years later, while preparing supper, she hears a truck pulling into the driveway. The tap of an airhorn brings three little kids to their feet, and they run out the door, hollering, "Momma, Daddy's home!"

A smile spread across Leann's face as she brushes back a tear. She can't help but remember that cold, miserable, rainy night on the roadside with a flat tire. Who would've ever thought it would be that night she obtained mercy and found grace to help in time of need—

not just for one night but for the rest of her life? In her mind, Brian was wrong about one thing. He was her knight in shining armor.

Hope is often born of desperation.

LOOKING FOR A PLACE TO CROSS

When thou passest through the waters,
I will be with thee; and through the rivers, they shall
not overflow thee.
— Isaiah 43:5 (KJV)

"The water's too deep, and I'm scared," exclaimed the terrified little girl as she sat sobbing by the river.

A friendly man approaching nearby responded, "Hi, Jacelyn. I'm Jerome, the crosswalk guard from school. I live down the river. Stick with me, and I'll help you get across." As they walked together by the river, Jacelyn's heart stopped beating so fast.

She'd seen him at school and knew his name, but not much else. Nevertheless, he was a calming presence to her troubled mind. Though she was cold and battered by the storm, she'd be home soon. After a few minutes of walking, they came to a spot that was shallow, even though the river was up a little higher than normal.

"Here it is," Jerome said. Tying his shoes together and throwing them over his shoulder, he reached for her hand.

"Take my hand. I promise I won't let you fall."

Her heart beat faster again as she studied the water, but holding Jerome's hand eased her fear.

Several steps later, they reached the other side through the rushing current.

"I told you we'd make it. I've walked across this river many times with lots of people. Sometimes it was much rougher than this. The key is knowing where the rocks are." Jerome saw her dad standing in the doorway, waved goodbye, and went on his way.

She joyfully ran across the field to her dad's waiting arms.

"Let's get out of the storm," he shouted, stooping to pick her up. "I've told you never to cross the river alone when it's storming."

"But Daddy, I wasn't alone!" Jacelyn said. "Jerome, the crosswalk guard from school, helped me across. He lives on down the river."

"But I saw you come up from the water, and no one was with you."

"Sure there was, Daddy. Jerome saw you and waved before he went on his way. I guess you didn't see him. He told me the key is knowing where the rocks are."

A little hope and faith can guide you through the worst of times.

DINING WITH THE BOSS

For as the heavens are higher than the earth,
so are my ways higher than your ways,
and my thoughts than your thoughts.
—Isaiah 55:9 (KJV)

Things had gone from bad to worse since Mick lost his job when the trailer manufacturing plant closed. His house had been foreclosed on, and living in his car with his family was the best he could do. He had started a new job as a maintenance assistant three months ago.

Hunger pains filled his belly as doubts filled his mind. Working at the governor's mansion sure seemed like the ideal job for Mick. He was a jack-of-all-trades and a master of none, as the old saying goes. He told everyone he walked to work each day for exercise because he was afraid if anyone found out he and his family were living in his car, he would lose his job.

The governor's limo pulled up the mansion driveway and stopped beside Mick. "I've never liked eating by myself. Come on up to the house at about 11:30, and we'll see what the cook can scrounge up."

"Thank you, sir. I'll be there." The governor had no way of knowing the pack of crackers in Mick's jacket was going to be his lunch. His family had to eat, so Mick had grown accustomed to doing without. Skipping lunch meant he could set aside a little more money for a deposit on an apartment before winter arrived.

Mick smiled. "Thank You, Lord. I knew you were listening." He lifted his hand in a wave toward the sky.

Walking into the mansion for the first time, Mick took in all its luxury. A voice behind him said, "Just in time. Our food will be out in a minute. I hope you like barbecue."

"Yes, sir," he said as the governor opened the patio door.

"Let's eat out here and enjoy this sunshine."

Mick couldn't believe the governor was wearing gym shorts and a T-shirt—plain as dirt and a likable somebody.

Mick was so hungry he could've eaten the southbound end of a northbound mule. As they ate, the governor asked Mick about his family. Like most dads, he bragged about his kids.

"I sure envy you," he said.

"How come, sir?"

"My daughters are away at college. It's been years, but I still miss the laughter and the sound of little feet running through the house. You're a blessed man. Your kids will be gone before you know it, so cherish every moment."

"Yes, sir," he responded. "I certainly do."

"Mick, I've been watching you, and there's something we need to talk about."

Oh no. Surely, he isn't going to fire me. I can't afford to lose this job. "What is it, sir?" he asked as he pushed the negative thoughts from his mind.

"I may be asking a lot, but our maintenance chief is retiring and moving to Florida. I need someone I can count on to take care of this place. The staff tells me you can do pretty much anything that needs doing, and you're the kind of man I need. What do you think, Mick?"

Before he could answer, the governor added, "One more thing you need to know before you decide."

"What's that, sir?"

"The maintenance chief lives on-premises, in a big house by the pond. Talk it over with your wife and let me know. You'll get a raise if you don't mind moving."

"I'm sure she'll say yes, sir," Mick said, trying to contain his excitement.

That weekend, Mick and his family moved in. Before crossing the threshold, they bowed and thanked God for providing for them. The kids ran through the house, thrilled to have a home again. Ann and Mick opened the back door to check out the fenced-in yard. On the carport sat a 4WD pickup with a note from the governor on the seat, along with the keys.

"The job comes with a truck. You'll need one. I've enclosed my card and cell number. Call or text me if you need anything. I hope the Mrs. likes the house."

Mick's heart was as full as his stomach had been when he left the governor's mansion the week before. *How could one man be so blessed? When God answers prayer, he doesn't mess around.*

Never give up on God.
He never gives up on you.

EMPTY BOTTLES

*Every man also to whom God hath given riches and
wealth, and hath given him power to eat thereof, and
to take his portion, and to rejoice in his labor; this is
the gift of God.*
—Ecclesiastes 5:19 (KJV)

"Hey, boss, look at this." Thomas picked up a bottle and wiped it
with his sleeve.

"You sure make a lot of noise for a little feller." Marvin examined
what Thomas had found. "Looks like an old wine or whiskey decanter.
Might bring a pretty penny from the right person."

This was the seventh house they had torn down to make way for
the new city auditorium in the middle of town. Demolition paid a little
more than farming, but not by much. With four kids and a wife at
home, Marvin took all the work he could find to feed his family.

Times were hard, and his family was as dirt poor as everyone else
they knew. You only get so many crops out of a piece of ground before
it stops producing. At least taking down old buildings would provide
a steady income through the winter months, and he could work inside
on the coldest days.

Marvin and Thomas were simple men, raised to be satisfied with
what they had. They were proud but not prideful. They believed in
giving a man an honest day's work for an honest day's pay.
Dismantling buildings was hard work and low pay, but they got to

keep the materials. Cheap lumber was always in demand and hard to come by as the city grew. They made more money selling the scraps than they did for demolition. Collecting and straightening bent nails for resale helped too. When they weren't demolishing something, they often helped neighbors build barns with the wood and tin they sold to them.

The country's economy rebounded slowly in the 1940s following World War II, which came on the heels of the Great Depression of the 1930s. Men did what they could to feed their families. Too much pride could starve a family.

After they gathered up the bottles that evening, they climbed into Marvin's beat-up truck for the twelve-mile ride home. They stopped by the mercantile shop to sell the bottles, which were worth enough to buy a twenty-five-pound sack of flour to split between them and a couple of cans of coffee. With a load of used lumber and the thoughts of gravy and biscuits for supper, they felt like two of the richest men around.

Marvin looked at Thomas and laughed while dodging the potholes through town. "You know what? It's kind of funny. We have an old house that someone thought was junk, and some old bottles that had been tossed aside and forgotten, and we're gonna make a decent lick off someone else's trash. Plus, they pay us to haul it away. Life is good even when it ain't."

One man's trash is another man's treasure.

SEVENTEEN CENTS

*Be of good courage, and he shall strengthen your
heart, all ye that hope in the Lord.*
—Psalm 31:24 (KJV)

"Please, be patient with me," Linda said to the cashier.

Monica forced a smile and said, "No problem."

Seventeen cents was holding up the line.

The folks in line behind Linda, although impatient, took pity on her because her two-year-old girl and four-year-old boy were crying. Monica's oldest child, Mia, was being a trooper and tried unsuccessfully to keep the little ones quiet.

Suddenly, a gentleman behind her handed the cashier a five-dollar bill and said, "Take it out of this and give her the change."

"Oh, thank you, sir! I know I've got it here somewhere." Linda told him, fighting back tears.

"No worries," the man replied. "You just take good care of those babies."

"Thanks again," Linda said. "I'm so sorry to hold you all up," she told the other shoppers in the line.

She was still wiping tears as she walked out the door into the cold night air. Since her husband had left two years ago, Linda had worked two jobs as she raised three kids. When she told him she was pregnant again, he decided he didn't want to be a dad anymore. When she refused an abortion, he filed for a divorce and left. No alimony, child support, or anything at all. She hadn't heard from him since.

The kids spent many nights sleeping in the back booth at a 24-hour restaurant while Linda worked. She lived with her mom, but it wasn't an ideal situation. Mom had been paralyzed below the waist from a car accident when Linda was a teenager. Between the two and four-year-olds and their grandma, Mia had far more responsibility than a six-year-old should ever have.

Linda's church family helped her stay sane. The young kids fought over who got to carry the babies into the church. One girl always walked Mia to her Sunday school class.

"Good morning, Ms. Linda." Granny Maxwell always asked, "How about I take one of those babies off your hands for a while? You need to take a break and enjoy the service." She wasn't related to anyone in the church, but everyone called her Granny anyway.

"Granny, you don't know how right you are," Linda responded with a hug.

As she sat down on the bench, she noticed a young stranger.

"Good morning, ma'am. I'm Steven Johnson. That's sure a passel of purty young'uns you have," he said. "Y'all should be proud."

"Thank you," Linda responded politely, trying to hide that she was enjoying adult male attention for a change. "I'm proud of them, but I'm not married anymore."

"That's a shame," Steven said. "Somebody doesn't know what he's missing watching those babies grow up."

"You're right," Linda agreed. Just then, the Sunday school teacher stood to open the class in prayer.

After the service, Linda gathered her things and started out with her pint-sized helpers once again carrying the babies.

"Hey, Ms. Linda. Hold up a second, please," Steven said, walking up to her. "I know being a single mom with three kids isn't easy."

Sensing she was about to be judged by this stranger, she said, "And what would you know about it?"

"Just what I saw my mom go through with us growing up. I always promised her if I ever had a chance to help a single mom, I'd do it in a heartbeat. I don't mean to be intrusive, but if you need anything done around the house, here's my card. Give me a call. I'll work for food. I'll bring it myself if I have to."

"I'm sorry. I shouldn't have been so rude. I'm just defensive about the comments people make. Baby factory is one of the worst. Thank you, Steven. I may take you up on that."

"You do that, and I'll bring the pizza. I know about the comments too. I've heard that one, and some are much worse. People said them about my mom. If you need anything, don't hesitate to call."

"I will," Linda replied, looking at his card. "Wait a minute!" she said. "I know you now. When I was seventeen cents short at the store a while back, you gave the cashier five dollars, then handed me the change."

"Yep, that was me," Steven grinned.

As time passed, this story became a romance and ended happily ever after. Linda and Steven became a family, and she finally found the devotion and love she had always craved for herself and the kids.

Fairy tales can come true.

THINGS WORTH MORE THAN MONEY

Eleven stories about things that are truly priceless.

"Money makes the world go round." Have you ever heard that statement? There's nothing wrong with making money, and we all need it to purchase what we want and need. We must have it to provide food, shelter, and transportation for our families.

The following stories illustrate many items and relationships that are worth more than money. They talk about everything from an old house to a sewing machine. They also portray the differences between the older and younger generations and how we can learn from one another. The peace of mind that comes from receiving good news and the value and importance of adoption. The beauty of solitude and traveling back in time to a better and simpler way of life. The admiration of a child and the example we show them with our lives are of utmost importance. The most crucial nourishment for a child isn't food or items that can be bought, but those that can't be purchased and are given from a heart of love. Among them are time spent with children, making them feel special and important, and a listening ear.

God holds our next breath and our next heartbeat. We have no control over them. What shape would we be in if He withheld either from us? They are worth far more than money.

Memories are also worth more than money, and the best ones are often made without one red cent in your pocket. The countless Friday nights I spent with my grandma when I was young are one example. Saturdays were often spent hunting with my brother and our best friends on the mountain behind her house. Once, I was taking a break from a walk with my best friend Stanley, and one shot from his gun stopped a snake slithering straight for me. Another time in my early twenties, I went up the mountain squirrel hunting by myself, then decided to go down the other side of the mountain and walk back to the community at the bottom. But along the way, I changed my mind and took another path back up the mountain. Two or three hours later, I reached the dirt road. I came out about five miles from where I started. A friend passing by with his family gave me a ride back down the mountain to Grandma's house. I didn't get any squirrels, but I got a lot of exercise.

When my family moved from our first house, I learned it was more valuable than the money we made from the sale of it. My wife and I started our life together there the day we were married. It was our son's first home. I looked around and saw many improvements I had made in the twelve years we lived there. The little old house the three of us had outgrown was filled with memories and love.

Many items and relationships are left behind with time but will always be cherished. I spent time with my son as I walked along and held the handlebars of his tricycle in the church parking lot beside our home. I was there the first day he got off the school bus. Those memories can't be duplicated or replaced. If I'd had a different job when he was born, I would have made more of those memories with him. Sometimes the needs in our lives make change necessary, but that should never decrease the value of the moments we must leave behind.

It's easy, especially today, to get caught up in the rat race we call life and forget what is most important. We have a saying down home that reminds us sometimes we need to "stop and smell the roses." "Stop wishing your life away" was another saying I always heard from my parents. Not a single moment wasted can ever be regained. Too often we rush through life and fail to appreciate what we have that is most precious. Besides, people are far more precious than possessions.

THIS OLD HOUSE

Let your conversation be without covetousness,
and be content with such things as ye have.
—Hebrews 13:5 (KJV)

Clayton was sitting on his porch one fine spring day when his nephew stopped by for a visit.

"Morning, Uncle Clayton. How are you today?" Toby slid into the rocker beside his uncle.

"Finer than frog hair split eight ways. You're looking right dapper this morning, Toby."

"I'm going to town for a job interview. If I get it, I'll be set for life. I'll have a big house, be able to buy my dream car, might even settle down and get married one day."

"That sounds pretty good. But what if you don't get it?"

"Haven't even thought about that, Uncle Clayton. Besides, the job's almost a sure thing. That's all I'll ever need to make me happy."

"So, without this job, you'll never have happiness. Is that what you're saying? You know money can never buy happiness."

"No, but it can sure make a good down payment on it." Tony grinned. "How come you're always so happy, Uncle Clayton? You live in this little old house. Nice but nothing fancy. You've driven the same pickup for most of my life. Don't you ever think about buying a new one?"

"Not really. It would sit in the same spot that one does and take up the same space. It would get me where I need to go, just like that one does. Why would I want a new one to do everything my old one does? The only thing I'd gain is another payment to make for what I already have that doesn't cost me any extra. I'm perfectly happy with my old junker. It's still a good truck and does everything I need it to do." Uncle Clayton turned his attention to his fields for a few moments. "Your dad taught you to drive in that old truck out in the back pasture."

"I hadn't thought of it like that." Toby looked as if a light bulb had just come on in his head.

"Me, your mom, and your Uncle Joe were all born and grew up in this house. I proposed to your Aunt Minnie right there on that porch swing. One of the first pictures your grandma took of your dad was in front of that snowball bush out in the yard when he took your mom to the senior prom. He asked her to marry him that night." He pointed to the street in front of the house. "You and all your cousins learned to ride bicycles out there after Sunday dinners. Hasn't ever been another house built that has those memories. A new one would only be sticks and stones without all of them."

"I see what you mean, Uncle Clayton. Our family has a lot of years and memories invested in this old house. I hope you always keep it … and your old truck."

It isn't the things you have that make your life rich,
but the people you share life with.

AN HEIRLOOM AND A HERITAGE

The aged women, likewise, that they be in behavior
as becometh holiness ...
That they may teach the young women to be sober,
to love their husbands, to love their children.
—Titus 2:3–4 (KJV)

"Hey, Grandma. I came to see if you could help me with my class project." Melanie gave her grandmother a tight hug.

"I'm always thrilled to see you, but I don't know how much help I can be," Grandma answered. "What's the project?"

'We're studying about the self-sufficiency of American pioneers in my history class. I'm supposed to make a pioneer woman's dress. My friend, Marcus, is making a model of a moonshine still."

"I don't know anything about making a still, but I can teach you how to make a dress. I have a little project you can help me with, too."

"What's that, Grandma? I'll do anything I can."

"It's a deal then. I'll teach you how to make the dress and bake cookies." A mischievous smile spread across her face.

"But I don't need to know how to bake cookies."

"Oh yes, you do, young lady. That's my project. I'm taking cookies to the nursing home tomorrow after church. I could do it myself, but you'll have a family one day, and they'll want cookies. Anything homemade from a cookie sheet is better than anything from a bag or a box. Besides, if you're learning about pioneer women, you'll learn they knew how to cook and sew."

"If you insist." Melanie knew her grandma had just suckered her in. "Check out this cookie recipe on my phone."

"My goodness, child. What kind of gadget will they come up with next? I've got a recipe book in the cabinet by the stove, but I don't need it either. I've got it all right here." Grandma pointed to her head. "It would've saved me a lot of writing if I'd had one of those gadgets back in my younger days. I bet that thing is as handy as a pocket on a shirt."

"No one writes notes anymore. We just keep everything in our phones." Melanie said, proud she could tell her grandma something too.

"Enough chatter. If we don't start baking, we won't ever get done. I'll even let you take me to the nursing home in your shiny red car."

Melanie enjoyed baking. She even asked Grandma to teach her how to cook other dishes. Most of all, she liked spending time with her and learning how to do things her grandmother had done as a girl.

Grandma and Melanie took the cookies to the nursing home the next afternoon. Grandma waved at her friends as she rode through town in the red Camaro. Melanie had forgotten how much fun she could have hanging out with her grandma and learning from her experience.

At the nursing home, Melanie was everybody's darling. All the ladies fussed over her, and the men talked about how pretty she was and how good the cookies were.

When they returned home, Grandma uncovered an old cabinet-looking table with a metal plate fastened to it near the floor. Melanie had never seen such a contraption. "What's that?"

"That, my dear, is my sewing machine. We'll use it to make your dress."

"We can't use that. It doesn't even have a cord to plug it in."

With a chuckle, Grandma replied, "It doesn't need one. That's what the pedal's for." She raised the lid, lifted the machine from inside the cabinet, and fastened it in place. Melanie stood mesmerized as Grandma placed a piece of cloth under the needle and pedaled the plate near the floor. The needle jumped up and down the faster she moved the pedal. When she stopped, Grandma handed the cloth to Melanie. "This is a row of stitches. They fasten two parts of the dress together. Now that you have an idea of what we're doing, we'll pick out some cloth and a pattern and get started on your dress."

Two weeks later, the dress was completed. Melanie's legs were sore from all the pedaling she had done.

Grandma wanted a picture of her granddaughter wearing the dress. "That dress looks beautiful on you, girl. I'm so proud of you. Someday, when I'm gone, I want you to have this old sewing machine. Your mom never took to it like you did. I hope one day you'll have some little girls to make dresses for and teach them to sew. You'll enjoy, as you young folks say, blowing their mind the first time they see the sewing machine, just like it did yours."

"Thanks, Grandma. I'll always treasure it because it came from you. Thanks for teaching me. I got an A+ on my class project, and I couldn't have done it without you."

Wisdom comes with age and experience.
Take time to listen and learn from older folks.

THE STICKY NOTES

She hath done what she could.
—Mark 14:8 (KJV)

"Twenty-four long agonizing days, and I finally get to blow this joint," Andy said as he packed his clothes to leave the hospital. At eighteen and a half, he was one of the youngest kidney transplant recipients in North Carolina Baptist Hospital's history. Doctors never fully determined why his kidneys had failed, but hopefully those days were behind him now. Thanks to his nineteen-year-old brother Jim, who donated his kidney, Andy's life would never be the same.

When Mom first told Jim the previous January about the upcoming surgery, he replied, "I've got two kidneys if he needs one. Just let me know when I need to take off from work to be tested." That major life decision from a nineteen-year-old was made in about three seconds as he smeared mayonnaise on a bologna sandwich. Jim had gotten home less than a week after donating his kidney to Andy and was almost fully recovered. When his kid brother arrived back home, Jim joked, "I didn't know you liked the hospital enough to stay that long."

This was a day of celebration. Not only was Andy going home with a working kidney, but it was also his mom and dad's twenty-first wedding anniversary.

"Mom, let's go up to the diner while we wait for Dad."

"Are you sure we have time?" Mom asked as Andy checked his

watch.

"Oh, yeah," he replied. "It's only been two hours since you called and told him I was discharged. It'll take at least another hour for him to get here, depending on the traffic."

Right then, they heard a horn blow behind them.

"Look, Mom. How in the world did Dad get here that fast?" Andy barely believed his eyes.

Dad pulled to the curb. "Are y'all ready to go home?"

"You better believe it, Dad. But we didn't expect you so soon."

"Let's just say I drove a little faster than I should have."

They all laughed as Andy and Mom got into the car. October had been a long month, but the surprises weren't over.

When they arrived home, Andy saw sticky notes on all the furniture. After hugging his two little sisters, whom he hadn't seen since leaving for the hospital, he asked, "What's all this?"

"Read them," his youngest sister Norma answered.

"It's amazing what you can do with a pack of sticky notes, a pencil, and determination to make someone feel loved," Robin chimed in.

Andy picked up a sticky note and read it out loud: "The chair missed you." Then he picked up another. "The table missed you." And another. "The TV missed you." Everywhere he looked, there were yellow sticky notes with the same message written on them. Robin and Norma had spent an hour or more writing these notes to let their big brother know he was missed.

There are many more details to Andy's story, but it's really about the sticky notes. Andy's sisters were fourteen and twelve at the time.

With no money or jobs, they wanted to find a way to let their brother know they missed him.

When you can't do anything else, do something nice.
Those moments make lasting memories.

POCKET CHANGE

And let us not be weary in well doing:
for in due season we shall reap, if we faint not.
—Galatians 6:9 (KJV)

Lela and Rachel burst into tears when their mom broke the news to them about Davis.

"He can't be paralyzed, he's too young," Lela said.

"It might only be temporary." Mom tried to sound confident for her daughter's sake. Davis had been their neighbor since Lela was born. He was three years older, but they had always been great friends.

"What happened?" Rachel asked.

"He was turning left and a drunk driver ran the red light and crashed into his car. The doctors hope it's just an inflamed nerve. Only time will tell," Mom explained. "His mom said you girls can visit him in the hospital anytime."

"Can we go tomorrow?" Lela asked.

"Yes, we can bake some cookies for him. Cookies always cheer anyone up," Mom said as she put on her apron.

"I have an idea, Mom. Can we bake stuff and have bake sales to raise money for his hospital bills and therapy?" Rachel asked.

"That's thoughtful of you, Rachel. Lela, are you going to help your sister?"

"You know I will. Davis has been our friend for as long as I can remember.

"It's settled then. We'll bake some for our visit, then tomorrow afternoon we'll get down to some serious baking. I'm sure people will buy some cookies and cakes to help out." Mom smiled. "I'm so proud of you two for wanting to do this."

Davis Wheatley beamed when Rachel, Lela, and their mom walked into his hospital room the following day.

"I'd stand up like a gentleman, but given the circumstances, I'll lie here and smile," Davis joked. "Is that your mom's chocolate chip cookies I smell?" he asked, staring at the dish Lela held.

"You always did like my cookies, Davis." Mrs. Randall smiled as she leaned over to hug him.

"Don't cry, girls," Davis said when their eyes teared up. "I'll be fine. You can't keep a good man down."

When they left the hospital, both girls burst into tears. "Mom, we've got to bake a lot of stuff to help him. I can't stand to see him like that," Rachel said, tears running down her cheeks.

"Me neither," Lela said, wiping her face with her sleeve.

In the coming weeks, the girls learned to bake very well. Their baked goods sold faster than they could make them.

After Davis came home from the hospital, the girls took him some cookies and an earthquake cake.

"Hey, girls. I smell something good," he said, sticking his nose up in the air and sniffing. "A little bird said you two were selling baked goods to raise money for me. Is that true?" He chomped a big bite of his cookie.

"I didn't know birds could talk, Davis," Lela shot back as she handed him a piece of the cake.

"You know what I mean, Lela. Rachel, are you going to tell me? You never could lie with a straight face."

"I still can't. You heard right, and here is five hundred and twenty-six dollars we've raised so far. Everyone is buying our cookies and cakes to help you. You have a lot of friends."

"Thanks, girls. I do have a lot of friends. You two are the best that a guy could ever hope for. This means more than you'll ever know," Davis said, swallowing a lump in his throat. "Even tough guys cry sometimes."

"Hey, watch this," Davis said as he locked the brakes on his wheelchair. He took a deep breath and pushed up with all his strength. "I'm not running yet, but standing is a good start."

"Wow, it was only temporary." Rachel started crying again—this time tears of joy.

Acts of kindness make a lasting friendship.

THE GREATEST PLAY

Let *nothing* be done *through strife or vainglory;*
but in lowliness of mind let each esteem other better
than themselves.
—Philippians 2:3 (KJV)

It was the last game of Marcy's senior season of basketball. She had been a star in the making until seventh grade. That's when her world changed forever.

"Hang on tight, kids. We're running off the road," the bus driver shouted. Twenty-three years of driving a bus with a clean record were gone in a flash as the bus careened off the road and into the ravine.

"Is everyone alright?" Sid yelled as he crawled across the bus seats. "Holler if you're okay." One by one, the kids all checked in. They'd been bounced from their seats when the bus flipped onto its side.

"We're missing one," Sid yelled. "Where's Marcy?" All the students began looking for her, then a sixth grader called out, "Coach. She's stuck under this seat, and she's not moving."

Sid crawled through the overturned bus to reach Marcy. He put his handkerchief on her forehead to stop the bleeding.

"Hey, Sid. Are you alright? What can I do to help?" hollered Lindon, the school's custodian, from outside the front of the bus. He'd seen the crash and stopped to help.

"Help the kids out and away from the bus. Call 911. Marcy's head is bleeding, and she's unconscious. She's breathing, but she's hurt bad." Sid slid his arm under Marcy's head.

Many people had gathered at the scene of the accident when Sid crawled out of the bus. After watching the EMTs load Marcy into the ambulance, he sat on the crumpled guardrail, burst into tears, and shook uncontrollably. Mr. Tompkins, the principal, walked over to him with a highway patrolman.

"Sid, are you hurt?" he asked.

"Just a little bruised up, sir. How are the kids, and is Marcy going to be okay?"

"They're fine. A little shaken up, but otherwise good. The paramedics said she'd lost a lot of blood and would've probably been a lot worse if you hadn't stopped her bleeding. The parents have already picked up the other kids, and Marcy's parents are meeting the ambulance at the hospital." Mr. Tompkins replied. "Sid, Trooper Miller has some questions for you."

"Okay," he said, wiping away tears.

"What happened, Sid?" the trooper asked.

"It was that high school girl with the red Corvette. I've seen her leaving the school before. She drives pretty reckless. She almost hit me when she swerved in front of the bus. I tried to miss her. That's when I hit the guardrail and cut the front tire. After that, I couldn't hold the bus steady, and it flipped over the rail. Is that girl hurt?"

"Did she even see you before the crash?" Trooper Miller asked.

"I don't think so. She was looking down when she hit us. How is she?" Sid asked again.

"She didn't make it. Her phone was in her hand. It appears she was texting and driving. But your actions saved a lot of kids here today. It would've been much worse if you hadn't been paying attention. Mr. Tompkins is waiting to take you to the hospital to be checked out."

Sid slumped into Mr. Tompkins's car, put his head in his hands, and sobbed like a hurt child.

"You did everything you could," the principal said, laying his hand on Sid's shoulder.

Five years later, Marcy still had a significant limp because of a shattered knee. She suffered some head trauma, and her reaction time was slower, but she still wanted to be on the basketball team. She was given a uniform, filled the water bottles, and kept fresh towels for the players. Coach Sid had become the team bus driver and coach for the high school.

In the team's last game that season, Coach Sid called a timeout with twenty-nine seconds to go. "Marcy, get in there. You can't spend your final moments as a basketball player on the bench."

Everyone in the gym rose and applauded when Marcy stepped onto the court. Even the opposing players approached her, giving her high-fives as she took her position. When the whistle blew, Marcy's team moved the ball down the court, slowly taking time off the clock. They were down by one point. When she passed the foul line, Lydia called her name.

"Here, Marcy. Shoot it," Lydia shouted as she passed to Marcy. When the ball hit her hands, Marcy threw it toward the basket. It rolled around the rim as the buzzer sounded and dropped through the net, giving her team the win. When she stopped to shoot, the visiting team stopped and watched Marcy drain the final shot of her career.

Marcy's shot may have won the game, but the other team, in a beautiful display of sportsmanship, let her shoot unopposed. Marcy wouldn't have been there if not for the actions of her coach five years earlier. So, who really made the greatest play?

Greatness isn't always what you do,
but often it's who you do it for.

BURIED TREASURE

A good man out of the treasure of his heart
bringeth forth that which is good.
—Luke 6:45 (KJV)

Sam Sneed was headed back to Cottonwood, his hometown. Now retired from the military, he'd been asked by his childhood neighbor, Mrs. Nolan, to visit her in the retirement home where she now lived. Her husband, Bernie, had passed away years before Sam retired.

"Sam," Mrs. Nolan said when he first walked in, "I need a favor."

"Yes, ma'am, I'll do anything I can to help you."

"I'm an old woman now, and my last wish is to see mine and Bernie's little farm again. Would you mind taking me there?"

"I'd be honored. When would you like to go?"

"I'm ready now, and I've already gotten approval from the staff," she said with a mischievous grin.

"Now is as good a time as any," Sam replied. "I'll get the car."

"Yes, you will," she told him. He attributed her unusual remark to her age.

At the old farm, Mrs. Nolan told Sam to park in front of the barn. Getting out of the car, she seemed to have a renewed vigor as she looked at him and said, "Follow me."

The spry old lady moved with a purpose and drive she probably hadn't had in years.

The rollers creaked like screeching train wheels when Sam pushed the barn door open. Between the windows Mr. Nolan put in when he built it and the sheets of the tin roof that had long since blown away, there was plenty of light to see what remained in the barn.

"Sam, everything here is yours if you'll clean it out for me. Sell it, keep it, or whatever— it's yours. No telling what antiques and old tools you'll find."

"I don't know what to say but thank you, Mrs. Nolan. Of course I'll take care of this for you," Sam replied, completely caught off guard by her request.

"One more thing. Pull that big tarp back and see what's buried under it. Do it kind of easy," she said.

Sam slowly pulled it back, then stopped. "You've got to be kidding me. Is this Mr. Bernie's old '56 T-Bird? I haven't seen it since I was a kid. I remember him raising the hood and talking about the 312 Overhead Valve V-8 power plant, sitting there like a pearl in an oyster. I didn't understand all he said, but I knew he was proud of his car." He pulled the tarp back a little more. "What am I supposed to do with it?" he asked as he gently wiped some dust from the hood. "It's fire engine red, just like I remembered. She sure is a beauty."

"Do what you want with it, but I hope you'll restore it and drive it. I knew it was here in the barn. Bernie would've wanted you to have it. He knew how much you liked it."

"But I can't accept that. It's too much."

"Yes, you can. You said you'd help me. No one else could appreciate and love that car as much as you. Besides, you're a man of your word, and you said you'd clean out everything in the barn." Mrs. Nolan flashed her mischievous grin once more.

As with anything that old, the car would require a lot of tender loving care. It would mean a lot of weeknights burning the midnight oil, even on Saturdays. But anything worth having requires a lot of time and effort. Sam didn't see that dirty bird under the tarp. He smiled as his mind went to the shiny red Thunderbird he had so admired as a boy. And now he would treasure it, just as Mr. Bernie had.

Anything worth having is worth working for.

GOING ANOTHER WAY

*And being warned of God in a dream that they
should not return to Herod, they departed into their
own country another way.*
—Matthew 2:12 (KJV)

Gary couldn't believe his rotten luck. He was already running behind, and the interstate was partially blocked by major bridge repairs. The traffic was already backed up for eleven miles and growing. That would probably delay him for at least a couple of hours. Climbing down from the cab, he looked up and groaned in frustration. "Why me and why today?"

Gary had only been to the little community of Upper Jaw a couple of times. He usually ran the interstate to Lower Jaw and took Highway 33 from the other end to Upper Jaw. But with the interstate blocked, he would have to take Highway 33 from this exit.

The little town of Upper Jaw takes a person back almost fifty years. No one locks their doors, and if someone sees a stranger come into town, they're apt to ask him to join them at the local diner for some good food and better conversation.

Signs warned truckers to choose another route, but there was no other route due to low clearances. He stared at the setting sun, wishing he hadn't accepted the load. But the job paid well, and he needed the money. Highway 33 was nineteen miles of bad road, and with about an hour until dark, he didn't have time to waste. He climbed in the cab and made the hard right turn onto the highway, which was little more than a paved pig trail through the woods.

I guess there are worse places a man could be than on this beautiful highway. The tension in his shoulders eased. Although the road was crooked and steep, being away from all the interstate traffic and construction was enjoyable. He chuckled as he thought about being in a time machine. He didn't know Peterbilt had made one, but on this old road, that's exactly what his truck was. It carried him back to a much simpler time.

Gary rounded the last curve an hour later. He stopped in front of the church, where there was plenty of room to park. Like an old pioneer village, this town had one church, a K–12 school, a country store, and a gas station with a garage and a mechanic.

When he parked, an older gentleman approached him with a smile. "After dragging that wagon across 33, I bet you're ready for some down-home cooking. I was headed to the diner. You're welcome to join me for a bite if you're not picky about the company you keep. I'm Claude Ray."

"Gary Thomas," he said as he stretched and stuck out his hand. "Nice to meet you, Mr. Ray."

"Oh no, son. Mr. Ray was my dad. I'm just Claude."

"Well, Claude, that diner is the best idea I've heard all day."

Unloading his truck at the country store the next morning, Gary met many of the locals who came to stock up on necessities. The store's owner, Jimmy Tomlin, carried about everything. They had a saying around town: "If Jimmy don't have it, you probably don't really need it."

The town survived on hospitality, hunting, fishing, and camping. Most of the men offered guide services, and all could skin a buck, bear, or clean fish with blinding speed. When Jimmy ran out of anything, he made the 47-mile trip down the other end of 33 to Lower Jaw.

Lower Jaw had a good logging industry and a big lumber mill that employed most of Upper Jaw's residents. The rest drove another thirteen miles to work near Pencilville, which got its name from all the lumber businesses there. About sixty years earlier, a visitor who saw all the logging and lumber businesses nearby joked that he bet half the pencils in the country came out of those woods. The joke stuck, and the town was named Pencilville.

After breakfast, Claude and Gary walked over to his truck.

"You need to come back for a fishing trip, young man. I know the perfect spot."

"That sounds like a winner, Claude." Gary handed him a business card. "Call me, and we'll make plans for it."

Waving goodbye, he headed toward Lower Jaw. Once there, turning onto the interstate, he thought about how blessed he was to have been forced to take SH33. He traveled back in time and met some of the nicest folks he could ever hope to meet.

You often find a lot of good in the world
by taking the road less traveled.

HANDPICKED

I have chosen you out of the world.
—John 15:19 (KJV)

"Why can't I have a home?" Jessica cried as Maria left with her new parents. "One day," Mrs. Stafford said. "Today was Maria's turn. Keep praying, and maybe it'll happen." Childlike faith is hard to muster when you've just watched your prayers answered for someone else.

But Mrs. Stafford was right. Two years, three months, and twenty-two days after giving Jessica that encouragement, it happened. Dreams can come true, and prayers still get answered. Joe and Sandra McBride were an average middle-aged couple when they came to the Little Blessings Children's Home. In their mid-thirties, they never had children. Health conditions and careers had gotten in the way. Now, they wanted a child to share their lives with.

"We're too old for a newborn, but we'd like an older child, maybe about nine years old," they told Mrs. Stafford. Although surprised, she knew right away who to introduce them to. Jessica was called to the office. She entered, her head hung in shame, certain it must be about her low test grade. As she closed the office door, she noticed Mr. and Mrs. McBride seated behind the door.

"Hi, Jessica," Mrs. McBride said. "How has your day been?"

"Fine. Are you folks here for a baby?"

"Not exactly," Mr. McBride smiled.

Something about his voice put Jessica at ease.

"We're looking for a young lady about your age to take home with us," he said. "Would you happen to know a good one?

"You bet I would. Let me get my things," she said, grabbing the door handle.

Suddenly, Jessica stopped and turned around. "I'm sorry, but I can't go with you. I can't leave my little brother Joey. He's only seven, and he needs me. I have to take care of him." Her voice shook as she held back her tears.

"Mrs. Stafford told us you'd say that, so we decided to take both of you. That is, if you still want to go," Mrs. McBride said.

"Yes, yes, yes," Jessica shouted, throwing her arms around their necks.

Mrs. Stafford then called Joey to the office. When he saw two strangers and the lady holding his sister close, he asked Mrs. Stafford, "What's going on, Jessica?"

Mrs. Stafford wiped away tears and said, "Joey, your day has come. Meet Joe and Sandra McBride, your new parents."

"Joey McBride. That has a nice ring to it. Hey, everyone will think I'm named after my dad, just like a normal kid," he said with a snaggletooth grin.

"You are a normal kid, son." Joe reached out to shake his hand. Joey ran past it and into his arms, giving him the biggest bear hug ever.

The McBrides had the usual struggles new families have. The kids still cried themselves to sleep sometimes, wondering why they couldn't have been born into a real family. One night, Sandra heard Joey sobbing and ran to his room.

"What's wrong, son?" she asked as Jessica ran in behind her to comfort him.

"Why couldn't we be born into a real family, like other kids are?" Joey asked through his tears.

"Oh, son, you're in a real family," answered Joe, coming into the room. "You two are extra special."

"How come?" Joey asked.

"That's simple. Other parents don't get to choose their kids; they take what they get. Your mom and I handpicked you and Jessica."

"Thanks, Dad." Joey sniffled, lying back on his pillow. "Hadn't ever thought of it like that."

When Joe and Sandra turned to leave, Jessica spoke up.

"Mom and Dad, we're sure glad you chose us."

Never stop believing.

THE OLD MAN AND THE ORPHAN

Hear counsel, and receive instruction,
that thou mayest be wise in thy latter end.
—Proverbs 19:20 (KJV)

Mrs. Murphy waved to the old gentleman sitting on the park bench as she opened the gate. She often brought the kids from the orphanage for an afternoon of play when the weather was good.

As young Timmy played, he watched the old gentleman sitting alone on the bench whistling a happy tune and whittling on a stick. Curious, Timmy pulled on his teacher's sweater. "Mrs. Applebee, who's that man?"

"That's Mr. Arthur. He used to teach at our school." She gathered the children around her and walked over to him. "Children, this is Mr. Arthur. He's a wonderful man and a friend to our school. Isn't his whistling beautiful?"

Timmy sat beside him and, as young boys do, asked, "What are you doing that for?"

"I'm talking to the birds."

"How do you do that?"

"I whistle a tune to them, and they whistle one back to me." Mr. Arthur turned back to his whittling. "Since my sweet Martha passed away, I come to this bench and talk to the birds and to God. I like to tell Him how beautiful His creation is." The old gentleman continued whittling his stick.

"What's that you're making?"

"Not sure yet. Looks more like a dog than anything else."

"A dog? How are you going to make that into a dog?"

"I'll whittle away everything that doesn't look like a dog."

As they talked, Timmy told Mr. Arthur about his life at the orphanage. He explained how his parents had died in a car crash and how, just like Mr. Arthur, he didn't have anyone. The old gentleman wiped a tear from his cheek and folded his knife closed. He handed Timmy the piece of wood.

"See, I told you it looked like a dog!" He gently bumped Timmy's shoulder.

"Wow. It was a dog the whole time, just like you said." Timmy twisted the wooden piece in his hand.

Time passed, and Timmy moved to middle school, but he continued to visit the park, where Mr. Arthur talked to the birds. On one visit, he pulled a piece of wood from his pocket and gave it to his friend.

"How do you like it?" Timmy asked. "I've been practicing, and I thought this piece of wood looked like a man on a park bench. I did like you said and whittled away everything that didn't look like that." Timmy beamed with pride. "I won first place in the art show at school with this carving. I owe you all the credit since you taught me how to whittle."

The old gentleman pondered for a moment, studying his gift with pleasure. "You know, Timmy, I have something for you, too." Mr.

Arthur reached into his pocket, pulled out his pocketknife, and handed it to his young friend.

Timmy's eyes widened. "Thanks, Mr. Arthur, but you need this."

"No, you take it. My hands ache so much these days I can hardly whittle anymore. Don't ever hurt anyone with it. Always use it to cut away whatever doesn't look like what you think it should be when you're whittling."

Mr. Arthur has long since passed. Timmy is married and has his own family. When he takes his boys to the park, he sits on Mr. Arthur's bench, where he spent many happy hours as a boy. He whittles while his youngest son looks on in amazement. As Timmy whittles, he whistles.

"What are you whistling about, Dad?"

"I'm talking to the birds, son. I whistle them a tune, and they whistle one back to me," he responds with a smile.

Time spent with a child is never wasted.

A CHEST FULL OF MEDALS

Thou therefore endure hardness,
as a good soldier of Jesus Christ.
—2 Timothy 2:3 (KJV)

"Momma, why does that man have all those shiny things on his coat?"

"He's a soldier, honey."

"What's a soldier, and what are they for?"

"A soldier fights evil, kind of like a superhero. Those shiny things are awards and medals he earned for his accomplishments and the battles he has been through."

"Why does he have so many?" Jake asked, as only a curious six-year-old boy can.

"Well, son, he has been a good soldier for a long time and has fought in several battles."

"Momma, when I'm big, can I be a good soldier like him and get me some medals?"

"Maybe you can, son." She ruffled his hair. "Right now, though, enjoy being a boy and having fun."

Harvey Raines, the soldier, saw Jake staring at his medals. He approached his mom and said, "Howdy, Ma'am. That's a fine-looking boy you got there. I overheard him asking you about my medals. Do you mind if I let him look closer, while I tell him about them?"

"That would be very kind of you. I'm trying to teach him not to stare, but I'm sure you know how curious six-year-old boys are." They both chucked.

"Yes, ma'am," he replied. "I used to be one, and I was just like him. That's how I wound up in this uniform. My dad was a decorated soldier and my hero. I got sucked in by his medals and his love for the country. I couldn't wait to get out of high school and join the military."

"Thank you for your service."

"It's my pleasure, and you're most welcome," Harvey said as he knelt and saluted.

"This is how we say hello and goodbye in the service," he explained. "So, what's your name, young man?"

"I'm Jake, and I'm gonna be a soldier just like you when I grow up. I'm going to get myself a uniform with shiny medals too."

"Is that right, son? I'm sure you'll make a fine soldier someday. But these medals don't come with the uniform."

"They don't," Jake asked with a perplexed look.

"Oh, no, sir," Harvey replied. "These medals are for a lot of different things. I had to work really hard to earn them. This one is for teaching young recruits how to survive and become good soldiers," he said, pointing to one in the center of them all. "These three are for some of the operations and battles I was involved in. These two are for jumping out of airplanes, and this one is for flying a helicopter."

"Wow," Jake replied. "But why would you jump out of an airplane?"

"That's what my boss, or my sergeant, told me to do. He said that was where I was supposed to get out, so I put a parachute on and jumped. That helped me float like a bird down to the ground."

"That sounds like fun. Just like the rides at Disneyland."

"Well, yeah. It's something like that. I hate to run, but my buddies are waiting for me. We have to get back to work before we get in trouble with the Sarge. You do good in school, and always mind your mom. When you're old enough, maybe you can sign up and get a job as a soldier." As Harvey stood tall and straight, he saluted Jake once again. Jake did the same, back to him, the best his little hand could do. With a smile and a tip of his hat to Jake's mom, he said, "Have a good day, ma'am. Thanks for letting me talk to your son. That's the most fun I've had all week."

"Thank you. You've made his day, and he'll be talking about you for a long time," she replied as Harvey turned to leave.

Always be the kind of person a parent
would want their child to look up to.

TWO MILES TO ETERNITY

Whereas ye know not what shall be on the morrow.
For what is your life? It is even a vapor, that
appeareth for a little time, and then vanisheth away.
—James 4:14 (KJV)

As the cold rain pounded him, Seaman Thomas pulled his overcoat around him tight, partially covering his face. Hitchhiking was a bad idea, especially on a night like this. Disheartened, he stuck out his thumb again as he saw headlights approaching. At long last, he got a ride.

As he slid into the warm car, the driver smiled and asked, "Where you headed, sailor?"

"A little town called Pickleberry, three hundred miles north," he replied, then thanked the gentleman for stopping.

"No problem. I'm Todd Johnson," he said as they shook hands. "Thank you for your service."

"I'm Jason Thomas, sir. You're welcome, and it's nice to meet you." Settling in for the long trip, he was thankful to be out of the rain and warm again. "This car's nice," he said, making conversation. "I don't think I've ever ridden in a Jaguar."

"Thanks, I like it, but repairs are expensive."

They passed the night away, talking like old friends. Six hours had flown by when they arrived at Jason's exit. The rain had stopped, and Todd got out to stretch and buy coffee at the roadside store. After thanking Todd again and talking a few more minutes, Jason crossed the road and walked up the long dirt driveway to his parent's home. Two weeks on leave would be a welcome break after four months at sea.

A few years later, when Jason was married and out of the Navy, he and his wife spent a week in New York City. Hanging up his overcoat, a business card fell from his pocket.

"Hey Miranda, look what I've found. This is the man who picked me up that time I was hitchhiking home on leave. I promised to look him up if I ever got to New York. Let's stop by his office. I want you to meet him."

The taxi pulled to the curb. When Jason and Miranda arrived on the fourteenth floor of the office building, he was eager to see Todd again. He asked the receptionist where he could find him. Looking confused, she asked, "Are you sure you're in the right place?"

"Sure, I'm sure," Jason replied, handing her the business card.

"Just a moment," she said and walked down the hall.

Moments later, she returned with another lady. "I'm Mrs. Johnson. Todd was my husband and the company president. How did you know him?"

"He picked me up once when I was hitchhiking home on leave from the Navy. I promised to look him up if I ever got here. What do you mean, was?" Jason asked.

"Todd died three years ago in a traffic accident. He was driving home when his car stalled several times and was hit by a passing motorist, killing him instantly."

"I'm so sorry," Jason replied. "I'll be praying for you."

"Thanks, but there's no need for that. I used to be a believer, but when Todd died, I quit church and gave up on God."

"Oh no, Mrs. Johnson. It was three years ago today that your husband picked me up. We got some coffee when he dropped me off at the Pickleberry exit, and we talked about the Lord before we parted ways." Jason smiled.

"Really?" Her voice broke and she began to cry.

"Yes," Jason assured her.

"You have no idea what a relief that is to hear. I guess the Lord was listening to my prayers after all. The accident happened two miles past your exit. I'm so glad you came to see him today."

"I am too. Most of all, I'm thankful God let our paths cross that night. I'm sure he had no idea it was only two miles to eternity."

Peace of mind is a precious gift that money can't buy.

JUDGING OTHERS

Seven stories showing the fallacy of judging others.

"What's wrong with that person? They shouldn't be acting like that." Have you ever thought that about someone? As a young man, I played for a church softball team. At the end of one game, a friend of mine threw his glove on the ground, then picked it up, and stomped off the field in a fit of rage. Two thoughts crossed my mind at that moment. The first was how my dad would kill me if he ever found out I acted that way. Then it dawned on me that we were a church softball team, and a Christian shouldn't be throwing a temper tantrum. I was embarrassed for my church, the boy's parents, and our whole team. I was almost twenty then, and decades later, I see my friend's angry outburst in my mind like it happened yesterday. We all have bad days and get frustrated with situations and even with ourselves. One's appearance or actions may not be a good representation of their normal character at all. Being much younger when that event happened, I was more judgmental than I should've been. Over time, I've concluded that we must be careful not to judge others based solely on one instance.

The next group of stories demonstrates that you can't always judge a book by its cover. I've heard it said that perception is reality. That is far from the truth. I've done mission work for a long time, and I've learned that what you see isn't always what you get. Underneath the ragged clothes or rough exterior lives a person with a heart and feelings, probably longing for acceptance like the rest of us. They can't be cast aside but must be shown God's love. They're some momma's baby and some daddy's little girl or boy. One thing they all have in common is the need for prayer and acceptance. Most of all, they are someone God gave His Son for.

We cannot possibly know the road someone has traveled to get where they are. We also have no way of knowing how we would respond in the same situation. People handle situations differently. What might make one person an emotional wreck will barely faze someone else.

These stories illustrate everything from overcoming difficult circumstances to empathizing with people who are struggling. Life can be hard. Most of us have hidden our pain behind a smile to avoid talking about hurtful situations with inquisitive people. Words can do a lot of damage, and they can never be taken back once spoken. They have consequences, and using them to pass judgment on others can be hurtful to the point of destroying lives.

How often has someone thought incorrectly about you because of a bad first impression or words you've spoken? If snide remarks and ill-willed comments hurt our feelings, they'll likely have the same effect on others. These stories demonstrate how wrong opinions often cloud our judgment.

The greatest king Israel ever had was nearly passed over because his father discounted him as nothing more than a shepherd. No one imagined David would become a valiant soldier, let alone the king who would rule over God's chosen people. Appearances can be deceitful, and first impressions can be wrong. David's father, Jesse, misjudged his son based on appearance and perceived ability. In the end, God equipped David for the purposes He had for his life. How many of David's brothers can you name? Probably none—a perfect example of how wrong our judgments can be. His brothers were mighty soldiers and looked the part. But David was the deliverer of his brothers and his countrymen when they faced Goliath. In 1 Samuel 13:14, the prophet told King Saul that God was removing him from the throne and had chosen David, a man after his own heart.

When we're tempted to look and discount someone based on their appearance or actions, we'd do well to remember David's story. We can't see anyone's heart, so we should refrain from judging others.

SCRAMBLED EGGS

Lo, children are an heritage of the Lord:
and the fruit of the womb is his reward.
—Psalm 127:3 (KJV)

Distraught and confused, Melanie shuffled to her car, wiping tears as she went. She was only seventeen. *I didn't think you could get pregnant the first time. What am I gonna do now?* Her situation had no easy answers. Each came with its own set of issues.

One thing was certain: she would not abort this baby. The Bible is plain about children. They're God's heritage. Jesus told His disciples to let the children come to Him. He then picked them up and blessed them. No way would she go against God. She would learn to be a mom earlier than she planned. One of her first hurdles: how would Chris take the news?

When Chris and Melanie met for their usual Friday night date, he could tell something was on her mind.

"What's wrong, babe?"

She cried as she told him they were going to be parents. With a look of disbelief, he pulled away.

"How?"

"Chris, you know how. There's only one way it happens! Aren't you excited? We're going to have a baby." Tears of joy and uncertainty flowed like a river down her rosy cheeks.

"I can't be a father right now. Scouts from the big colleges are looking at me for scholarships. I'm gonna pitch in the majors. I love you, Melanie, but no. I'm sorry."

Giving her back the chain with her class ring, he got up from the booth, bent over and kissed her forehead, and once again whispered, "I do love you." Handing him back his ring, she watched as he turned, put it on his finger, and left the restaurant.

A few minutes later, she got into her car and headed home. Chris's words rang hollow in her ears.

Walking away isn't love. Her tears came like a flood again. *I've always been good and stayed in church, and now this.* "Little one," Melanie said, wiping away tears and rubbing her belly. "Looks like it's gonna be you and me against the world. God will help us, and we'll make it no matter how hard it gets."

When Melanie arrived home, she walked in and said, "Mom, Dad, I need to talk to you." The words had come so easy on the way home as she rehearsed them, but now, it was almost like she had developed lockjaw.

"I'm pregnant," she blurted out as the tears flowed again. Immediately, her mom came over and hugged her. No words were spoken for a few minutes. Melanie watched her dad stare out the window and wipe tears. When he regained his composure, he turned and walked to her with his arms outstretched. She saw the disappointment in his eyes but also felt the love in his strong embrace.

"Baby girl," he said, gently brushing her cheek, "we'll get through this. Looks like we've got a young'un to raise. Now, we must focus on giving it all the love we possibly can."

We all mess up and sin, but God still forgives
and gives grace to the humble.

THINGS AREN'T ALWAYS WHAT THEY SEEM

Man looketh on the outward appearance,
but the Lord looketh on the heart.
—1 Samuel 16:7 (KJV)

The chilly rain pelted Everette as he walked down the muddy edge of the road. He shivered and pulled his collar up tighter. His clothes were ragged and dirty, but that was to be expected. Living like this, staying clean and presentable wasn't possible.

Since the mill closed three years ago, times had been hard. He had supervised over twenty people in what seemed like a past life. The money had been good and life even better. The pickup truck he'd been so proud of was now a distant memory. The bank had repossessed it two and a half years earlier.

Many of his old friends were gone, too. The mill closing devastated the town. He could've transferred to Mexico and kept his job, but he would've made far less money than here in his hometown. If the mill moved again, he'd be stuck in southern Mexico, where he couldn't speak the language and crime was rampant. He had cut his losses and stayed put. At least here, Everette knew the streets and what few people remained. That was much better than not knowing anyone in a strange place hundreds of miles away.

The reality of things became apparent when the rug got yanked out from under him. Poverty and tough times make anyone appreciate what little they still have. It also makes anybody more aware of others' needs. A quest for survival takes the place of greed, and while it may be miserable at times, it comes with a certain peace of mind.

Everette walked along whistling, and the rain started to fall harder. The cool fall air had a bite to it that chilled him to the bone when the wind blew. He picked up his pace and headed toward a nearby house. It was small, but he was sure he could get out of the rain and probably even get a bite to eat.

After a minute that seemed like forever to Everette in the rain, a woman unlocks and opens the door. She rushes him in, taking his coat while asking if he's hungry. Offering him a hot plate of mashed potatoes and gravy, onion, soup beans, and cornbread, she tells him to take a seat at the table. Before sitting, he puts his lunchbox on the counter, slips off his muddy boots, and puts them over a heat vent to dry until morning. He then steps to the kitchen sink and washes his hands.

Life may not be like it used to be, but it isn't as bad as it could be. Walking two miles from work isn't such a big deal. At least now he is warm, getting dry, and eating a hot meal. He counts his blessings, knowing he has more than many folks. He'll be warm and dry tonight, but he'll put his boots on before daylight tomorrow and walk the two miles back to work.

Many people passing him that evening may have thought he was some poor, lazy bum, judging by his dirty clothes. However, Everette is rich beyond compare and content with the Lord's blessings.

The place he stays each night isn't a shelter but his home. The food doesn't come from a soup kitchen but from his own, prepared by his devoted wife. Those things and his two young children make his daily trips in all kinds of weather worthwhile. The best part is both kids are too young to know how hard things are.

No, Everette isn't begging for handouts. He walks to and from work, so his wife has the car for emergencies. His clothes are usually filthy and ragged because he gets covered in black rubber working in a tire shop.

Things aren't always what they seem.

NOT GOOD ENOUGH TO COME IN

Come unto me, all ye that labor and are heavy
laden, and I will give you rest.
—Matthew 11:28 (KJV)

"You can't come in here looking like that, especially when you've not bathed in God only knows how long." The pastor's words stung Alfred to the core.

"I thought God's house was supposed to be a welcoming place where everyone is accepted," he said.

"It is. But you need to get cleaned up and act like somebody your momma would be proud of. Then you can come back."

Recognizing his concerns fell on deaf and judgmental ears, Alfred turned to leave. He was used to that kind of judgment. His arthritis had gotten so bad he could no longer work. *I guess when you're no longer useful and put out to pasture, what you did in the past doesn't matter.*

Shuffling across the street, Alfred headed down Zimmerman's Alley beside the furniture store. Finding a comfortable spot on the ground, he sat and leaned back against the wall. Reaching into his backpack, he pulled out an old, worn Bible.

"This old Bible is a lot like me, Lord. Rough around the edges, nearly worn out, and barely holding together. I reckon I've put it through a right smart, but it's gotten me through even more. When my

Martha and the kids died in a trainwreck on their way home that Christmas, I wouldn't have gotten through it if not for You and Your Word. I still don't understand why You took them, Lord, but I'll keep trusting You. You've never let me down yet, and I know You never will."

Alfred closed his Bible and drifted to sleep. Anyone passing by could've seen a slight smile on his weathered, wrinkled face. He dreamt of a time long since past when a man wasn't judged so much by his clothes as by his heart and his character. No one at the church remembered him. They were just babies when his family died, and he drifted away from the Lord. Back then, the congregation welcomed him with open arms. They showered him with love when they saw him out anywhere, not the slightest hint of judgment. Although they hadn't endured the heartache and loss he'd suffered, their hearts hurt with him.

A raindrop on his face woke him from his dream. He harbored no malice toward the young pastor. He bowed his head once more. "Lord, I pray that one day You'll let the pastor see what it's like to be part of a real, loving church family. I'm thankful I know what it's like."

Alfred slowly got to his feet, rubbing the sleep from his eyes. He strolled back through town, longing for the warmth and acceptance he had received years before.

"Lord, I can't help but wonder how many broken people they're turning away from their building and from You by their lack of compassion. Martha would be heartbroken to see what's going on now."

Stepping off the sidewalk to cross the street, Alfred looked back at the church again.

When he got to the other side, someone called his name.

"Alfred, is that you? It is you," the man said with the excitement of a kid at Christmas. "I've wondered what happened to you.

"How do you know me?" Alfred asked as the young man reached to shake his hand.

"I'm Jake Redmon. I was a young deacon at the church years ago. That rockwork you did looks as good as the day you laid it. I left town for a new job right before your family died. I was so sorry to hear about that."

"Thanks, young man. That was a long time ago, and some painful memories," Alfred responded as his eyes started to water.

"I've got an idea. Why don't we go to the diner and do some catching up? My treat. You inspired me to become a rock mason. When I saw what you did at the church, I decided right then that I had to learn to create a work of art with my hands like you did. Masonry has given me a good living for a lot of years. The least I can do is buy your lunch."

"I inspired you? No one's ever said that to me before, but I'd sure like to take you up on going to the diner. I'd be honored to break bread with you, young man."

Don't be quick to judge.
You never know the road someone has traveled.

WHICH WAY NOW?

And Samuel said unto Jesse, Are here all thy children? And he said, There remaineth yet the youngest, and, behold, he keepeth the sheep.
—1 Samuel 16:11 (KJV)

"We can't drive through a flooded road, and I'm new here. I don't know where to go," the bus driver said.

"Well, don't look at me, I've only lived here two months. I don't know either," replied the teacher, Ms. McConnell. "We don't have cell service. We can't call the school. What are we gonna do?"

"Turn left at the next road," Tyler said.

"How would you know that?" the driver replied.

"I saw it on a website," he said.

"Mrs. Jarvis, Tyler's autistic. We can't take his word for it," Ms. McConnell said. Turning to Tyler, she added, "Go back to your seat and be quiet, so Mrs. Jarvis and I can figure this out."

"Turn left," he said again, frustrated. "All you gotta do is turn left," he mumbled as he went back to his seat.

"I guess we can try it, Mrs. Jarvis. If we don't, I'm afraid he'll have a meltdown, and we don't want that."

"You're the boss, but I don't like the idea of a ten-year-old autistic kid giving me directions."

"Me neither, but I don't know what else to do. We can't sit here. If the water rises anymore, we'll be in serious trouble," Ms. McConnell said.

With their course of action determined, Mrs. Jarvis pulled forward and turned left onto Cherry Street Extension.

"I sure wish I knew where I was going," she said.

"There, there, there, turn right on Old Silo Road," Tyler said. "Then, turn left on Pinecone Lane." His voice grew louder and more insistent.

"Ms. McConnell, do you see what I see?" Mrs. Jarvis asked.

"Is that the interstate? We've only been four miles. Good job, Tyler," she said as she patted him on the shoulder. "But, how did you know that?"

"The County Roads website. We're getting on at Exit 127. The school is Exit 135, then turn left. The school is on the right."

"Tyler, I'm impressed. Maybe you should ride with me all the time, so I can learn my way around." Mrs. Jarvis looked up in her mirror and smiled at him.

When they got to the school, Principal Capps met them at the school's main entrance along with worried parents. "Where have you been? We were worried when we heard the old river road had flooded," he told Mrs. Jarvis.

She explained their ordeal to the worried parents who rushed over to get their kids. The other kids, who had been crying, cheered and patted Tyler on the back as they filed off the bus.

"There's Tyler, Momma. He gave Mrs. Jarvis directions and got us back here," one kid said. Hearing that, all the parents came over and gave Tyler high-fives, thanking him for getting their children back safely.

The following day at school, Principal Capps announced what had happened on the intercom and said Tyler was a hero because he had given directions that got the busload of kids back to the school. For the rest of the day, teachers and students throughout the school patted him on the back and told him what a good job he had done.

Don't overlook anyone.
Their gifts and abilities might make a difference in your life.

TWENTY-ONE CENTS

Thy tongue deviseth mischiefs;
like a sharp razor, working deceitfully.
—Psalm 52:2 (KJV)

Rhonda burst into tears as the man insulted her. Twenty-one cents had ruined her day. That's the amount the man was short on his groceries. If her purse hadn't been in the breakroom, she would've given the man the money. She had already been warned and written up twice for her drawer not being balanced. One more reprimand, and she'd lose her job.

She was soft-hearted to a fault and had let a single mom with three kids and an elderly lady without enough money leave without paying the full amount. Rhonda planned to make up the difference in both cases, but her boss refused to let her, even though she explained her reasons.

She simply couldn't afford to lose this job. Her mom, dying of cancer, had only months to live. Rhonda's eleven-year-old sister helped around the house some, but most of the responsibility fell on Rhonda's shoulders.

Life was hard enough, and this man felt the need to insult her because he didn't have enough money for a candy bar. She had been as pleasant as possible and had rung up his items twice at his insistence. When the amount came up the same, the man slammed the candy bar down on the counter, mouthed off because she wouldn't let him have it, and stormed out, cursing.

Rhonda left her register and ran to the restroom. She couldn't hold back the tears as she flung open the door. She bent down, laid her head on the sink counter, and sobbed uncontrollably. Sixteen-year-old girls should be thinking of prom and boys. Instead, she only thought about work, her mom, and how she could try to fill her mom's role with Angela when her mom passed. To be belittled over twenty-one cents was more than she could take.

Why must people be so mean over petty stuff? The issues she faced were overwhelming and almost unbearable. She tried to be strong for her mom and Angela. The man may have had a terrible day, but he should've shown some consideration for her. All this over a lousy candy bar and twenty-one cents.

That night in the store was a low point for Rhonda. Life began looking up slowly but surely in the next few weeks. Her boss was replaced by a young mom in her twenties who loved people. She doted on her employees, Rhonda in particular. She was as flexible with scheduling as Rhonda needed her to be for her mom's doctor appointments and treatments.

One of the treatments was still somewhat experimental, but her mom was accepted for the clinical trial. They paid her for participating in addition to paying for her medicines.

If that wasn't enough, Brian Meadows asked Rhonda to the prom. With her additional income from the clinical trial, her mom insisted she go. She even mustered up the strength to go with Rhonda to buy a prom dress. At least for one magical night, Rhonda could be a typical teenage girl.

With mom's health improving and the much-needed financial relief, life became somewhat normal again. Angela, once withdrawn, now had a closeness with her mom that only surviving hard times together can explain.

Rhonda kept her job at the store and was always mindful of how she talked to people. The encounter with the angry customer months earlier taught her that sticks and stones may break bones, but words spoken in anger can break someone's spirit. Bruises and bones heal, but the wounds from words often last a lifetime.

Choose your words carefully.
Once spoken, they can never be returned or forgotten.

A MAN NAMED CLYDE

Give, and it shall be given unto you, good measure,
Pressed down, and shaken together,
And running over.
—Matthew 25:35 (KJV)

One of my fondest childhood memories is about an old black gentleman in our town. He knew and loved everyone. I never heard anyone say a bad word about him. Clyde worked at the corner grocery store and pushed Mom's buggy to our house. He told her she had plenty to do, taking care of the baby and us boys. Mom always gave him a couple of dollars for his help. If I had pushed a buggy of groceries six blocks, it would've been worth every bit of two dollars or more.

Clyde's family was the first black family in town. People weren't as good and cordial as they are now, but Clyde never complained. His dad died of cancer when Clyde was young, and his mom had a sudden heart attack when he was in his teens. Clyde survived by doing odd jobs for anyone who would let him work, along with his job at the store. He had nothing to his name except a small apartment.

Tragedy seemed to hang over him like a dark cloud. His wife and daughter had been killed years earlier when a drunk driver ran his car onto the sidewalk in front of the store where Clyde now worked. Every day he walked past the spot where his whole world had been suddenly taken from him.

Clyde spent nearly a year trying to pull out of that dark time, but since then, he has been a new man. I asked him once why he was so nice to everybody and always smiled and tipped his hat. He smiled, rubbed my head, and said his life hadn't always been so good. Everyone in town had come to his aid at a time when he needed them the most. Then, with a puff on his pipe, he said, "Son, the good Lawd 'spects us to do others likes we wants them to do us. I's jus' trying to stay on his good side."

When I got older and started driving, I noticed Clyde walking all over town collecting cans in his spare time. I didn't think he needed money because he had no car. His apartment was a room built on the back of the church. The church folk had built it for him after his family was killed. People carried meals to him and fixed extras when cooking for their family so they had enough to take to Clyde. He became a fixture in the church and, with God's grace, pulled himself together.

After selling his cans, Clyde returned to the store and bought some canned food, bread, juice, and a little bag of Reese's Cups. I followed him as he also picked up a bottle of the raunchiest cough syrup known to man. It worked, but it made your teeth and tongue want to find a new home.

I noticed Clyde always left the store and headed in the opposite direction from his apartment. Curiosity got the best of me, so I followed him in my car at a distance. I guess I just wanted to see what made ol' Clyde tick. He crossed the railroad tracks and went underneath the bridge. A little brown-haired girl crawled down from the concrete ledge of the bridge and gave Clyde the biggest hug her little arms could give. Looking closer, I saw a bunch of cardboard and some old, ragged blankets and quilts someone must have pulled from a dumpster. Then the covers moved, and a woman sat up from underneath them. Sitting out of sight a little way off, I watched as Clyde sat down beside her, reached into the bag, pulled out the bottle of cough syrup, and opened it for the woman to take a swig.

I found out what I came for but could never tell what I saw. This little girl was in kindergarten, and Clyde sold cans to buy the stuff she needed for school. He also kept her and the woman in groceries and medicine when needed. As I moved a little closer, still staying out of sight, the woman thanked Clyde through a river of tears for all he was doing for her and her granddaughter. They both knew if social services found out about her living conditions, they would take the girl from her.

Clyde took the lady's hand, patted it, and said, "I knows what it's like to lose and keep losin' until everythin's gone."

I returned to my car, blinded by tears. Clyde wasn't an old man hoarding money. He gave it away as fast as he got it. He spent his life and money helping others, like people had helped him years earlier. I understood why he had taken the money from Mom. I had just seen an example of what godly love looks like—a smiling, old, black gentleman with a huge heart for others. Like a man named Clyde.

Do unto others as you would have them do unto you.

HERO AT THE FLAGPOLE

And Jephthah said unto the elders of Gilead,
Did not ye hate me, and expel me out of my father's
house? And why are ye come unto me now when ye
are in distress?
—Judges 11:7 (KJV)

It was a typical day in the southern Nevada desert. The school was immaculate because the school board was coming that afternoon for a meeting. Everyone on the administrative staff met in the principal's conference room to await their arrival. Without warning, a frantic call came over the walkie-talkie.

"You're not going to bloody believe this," Mrs. Reynolds, the custodian, blurted out. "This cannot be happening. Ms. Hutchins, you need to come out here to the flagpole."

Mrs. Reynolds wasn't one to get excited, but when she did, her distinct English accent became more pronounced. When Ms. Hutchins came around the building, she couldn't believe her eyes. With only an hour until the school board arrived, a girl was handcuffed to the flagpole, and the temperature was over 100 degrees and climbing.

Ms. Hutchins, a devout Christian, threw up a 911 prayer for divine assistance. It was an urgent request from her sincere heart because she was clueless about what to do. Just as quickly, the answer came: Call Billy.

Billy had been suspended the previous week. Ms. Hutchins had her secretary call and ask if he could come to the school, promising to lift his suspension if he came.

Moments later, an old, beat-up pickup pulled to a stop in front of the school, brakes scrubbing and the engine smoking. Billy slid out of his dad's truck and calmly strolled over to Ms. Hutchins.

"Why did you call me? I thought I was suspended until next Tuesday." He crossed his arms and waited for an explanation.

"You were, but since you came, I will lift it. I need your help. Missy said her ex-boyfriend, Stewart, handcuffed her to the flagpole when she broke up with him. Then he threw the key in the middle of the cactus patch. We've had rattlers and who knows what else in there in the past, so we don't dare try to find the key. Can you open a set of handcuffs?"

"Does anyone have a hairpin?" Billy looked around, as calm as the bottom side of a pillow.

When the administrative staff, janitor, and curious teachers told him no, he said, "A couple of paperclips might work."

The secretary ran to the office and returned in a few minutes. She handed the paper clips to Billy and stood with her mouth open when he handed them back to her in less than a minute.

Missy was sweating profusely, even though her teacher had held an umbrella over her to shield her from the blistering Nevada sun. She rubbed her wrists, then grabbed Billy around the neck and kissed him.

"Thanks, Billy. I thought I was going to die handcuffed to the flagpole." She wiped her face with a cold cloth the custodian had brought to help cool her off in the hot desert sun.

"Piece of cake, but you're welcome. The kiss wasn't bad either." His face turned red, but not from the heat.

"Billy, you're amazing," Ms. Hutchins said. "Where did you learn to do that?"

"Did you forget my dad is a locksmith? I guess I've picked up a few tricks along the way."

"I had forgotten," Ms. Hutchins replied. She looked at her watch. "I hate to run, but I've got a meeting with the school board soon. First, Stewart and I are going to have a come-to-Jesus meeting in my office. He'll be suspended for three days, but you can come back tomorrow, Billy. Thanks again for your help. I would've never thought someone who gets in as much trouble as you would bail me out when I needed it most."

"Just goes to show you, there's a little good in nearly everyone." Billy laughed as he climbed back into his dad's truck. "Even me."

Don't let your past determine your future.

ACKNOWLEDGEMENTS

I want to thank Cindy Sproles of christiandevotions.us and Beth Patch of CBN.org, respectively, who gave me my first opportunities to write devotions and believed in me. To Starr Ayers, who invited me to contribute three stories in two days to the award-winning book, Room At The Table. Finally, to my friend and publisher, Dr. Katherine Hutchinson Hayes, who invited me to write devotions for men for a new segment on her website called The Man Cave. That has grown into an ongoing and evolving project. Also, I've been blessed to contribute several pieces to her two compilation books. Focus: 45 Devotionals To Keep Jesus In The Picture, and Mountains Moved: 45 Devotions On Bold Faith, and another upcoming compilation with an incredible group of writers. All of these are available on Amazon and Kindle.

I owe all of you who gave me a chance to write a debt of gratitude I can never repay. My prayer is that God will richly bless each of you as you have blessed me. My goal is to spread the gospel and make each of you proud and thankful that you took a chance and believed in me.

Andy Hollifield is a published, multi-award-winning author with devotions appearing on the ChristianDevotions.us website and the CBN.com website. He is a contributing author to "Room at the Table." His upcoming book, *Breaking Point: Stories to Keep You Going Despite Impossible Odds*, is scheduled for release in the summer of 2026. Andy's website is www.downhome.media, and he hosts a weekly podcast called "Down Home with Uncle Andy" on Fridays from 6:00 to 6:15 p.m. on Riverside FM. He also contributes to Dr. Katherine Hutchinson-Hayes' award-winning devotional books—*Focus, Mountains Moved*, and *From Ruins to Restoration*—and writes regularly for "The Man Cave" (devotions by men for men) on her website www.drkatherinehayes.com.

Connect with Andy:

www.facebook.com/AndrewMHollifield

www.downhome.media

Coming 2026:

Breaking Point: Stories to Keep You Going Despite Impossible Odds